KU-033-491

MICHELIN

MINI-ATLAS

THE WORLD

Projection : Van der Grinten adapted by MICHELIN

Scale 1:28 500 000 at the Equator { 1 inch : 450 miles / 1 cm : 285 km

Capitals of independent states	● **Paris**
Capitals of federal states, provinces or territories	○ **Boston**
International state boundaries	- - - - - - - -
Boundaries of federal states, provinces or territories	....
Cities or urban areas of over 5 000 000 inhabitants	○
Towns and cities of over 1 000 000 inhabitants	○
Other towns and cities	○ ○
Roads - Tracks	—— - - - -
Transcontinental railways	——
Antarctic research station	▪
Altitude - Depth (in metres)	.4807 .5200
Coral reef	⬭

KEY TO MAP PAGES

A	B	A	B
C	D	C	D

For the purposes of indexing, each page is divided into four imaginary boxes — A, B, C, D — as shown here.

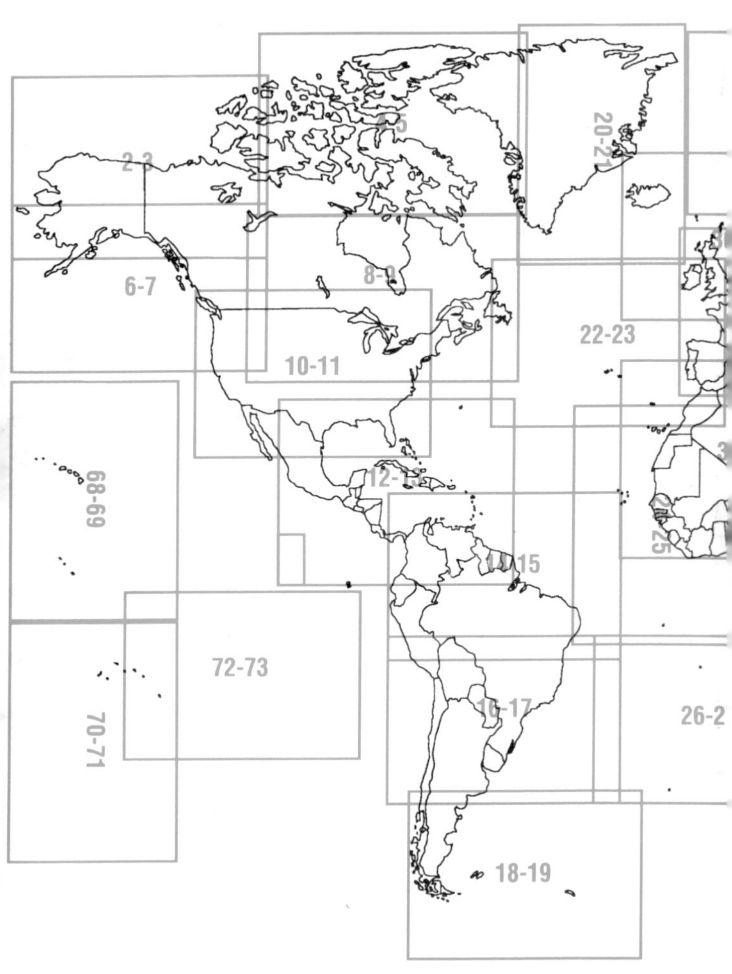

For the purposes of indexing, each page is divided into four imaginary boxes — A, B, C, D — as shown here.

A	B	A	B
C	D	C	D

KEY TO MAP PAGES

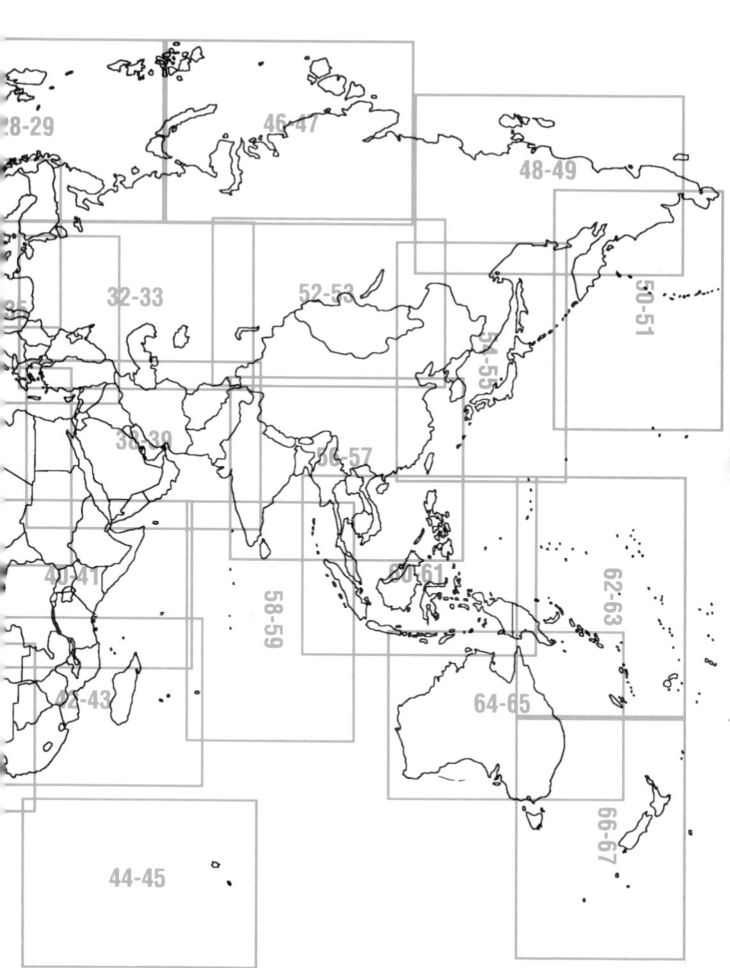

O. Vrangel'a
M. Šelagskij
Proliv Longa
Chukchi Sea
50
Poin
Brooks
Kotzebue
Kotzebue Sd.
Čukotskij P-ov
Uelen
Bering Strait
Wales
Providenija
Nome
(U.S.A.)
ALASKA
Tanana
Yukon
Norton Sound
Unalakleet
Lawrence I.
Fairbanks
Alaska
Range
6195
Mt. McKiniey
Tok
Bethel
Kuskokwim
ivak I.
Anchorage
Valdez
Cook Inlet
Seward
Homer
Naknek
Montague I.
Bay
59

Beaufort Sea
Sachs Harbour
C. Bathurst
Amundsen
Tuktoyaktuk
Inuvik
Porcupine
Fort Yukon
Fort McPherson
Fort Good Hope
Coppermin
Great Bear Lake
Mackenzie
Mackenzie Mountains
Dawson
YUKON
Mayo
Yukon
TERRITORY
NORTH
Whitehorse
Fort Simpson
Fort Providence
Yellowknife

QUEEN
Borden I.
Brock I.
Prince Patrick I.
Mackenzie King I.
Emerald I.
Hazen Str.
Lougheed I.
Eglinton I.
M'Clure Strait
PARRY ISL
Melville I.
Banks I.
Byam Martin I.
Viscount Melville Sound
Stefansson I.
VICTORIA ISLAND
M'Clintock Channel
Prince of Wales I.
Boothia Pen.
Cambridge Bay
Coppermine
Coronation G.
King William I.
Spence Bay
Queen Maud G.
Bathurst Inlet
Arctic Circle
Wales I.
Garry L.
THWEST TERRITORIES
Baker Lake
Dubawnt L.
Baker L.
Fort Reliance

Meighen I.
Peary Channel
Nansen Sd.
2926
Sverdrup Islands
Axel Heiberg I.
ELLESMERE
A. Ringnes I.
Cornwall I.
Graham I.
Belcher Channel
Knud
Qaanaaq (Thule)
Jones Sound
Devon I.
1887
Coburg I.
Lancaster Sound
Kap York
Melville Bugt
Brodeur Pen.
Arctic Bay
Bylot I.
Pond Inlet
Baffin Bay
BAFFIN ISLAND
Pen.
Rowley I.
Disko
Qeqertarsuaq (Godhavn)
Aasiaat (Egedesminde)
Prince Charles I.
Foxe Basin
2591
Davis
Strait
Sisimiut (Holsteinsborg)
Pangnirtung

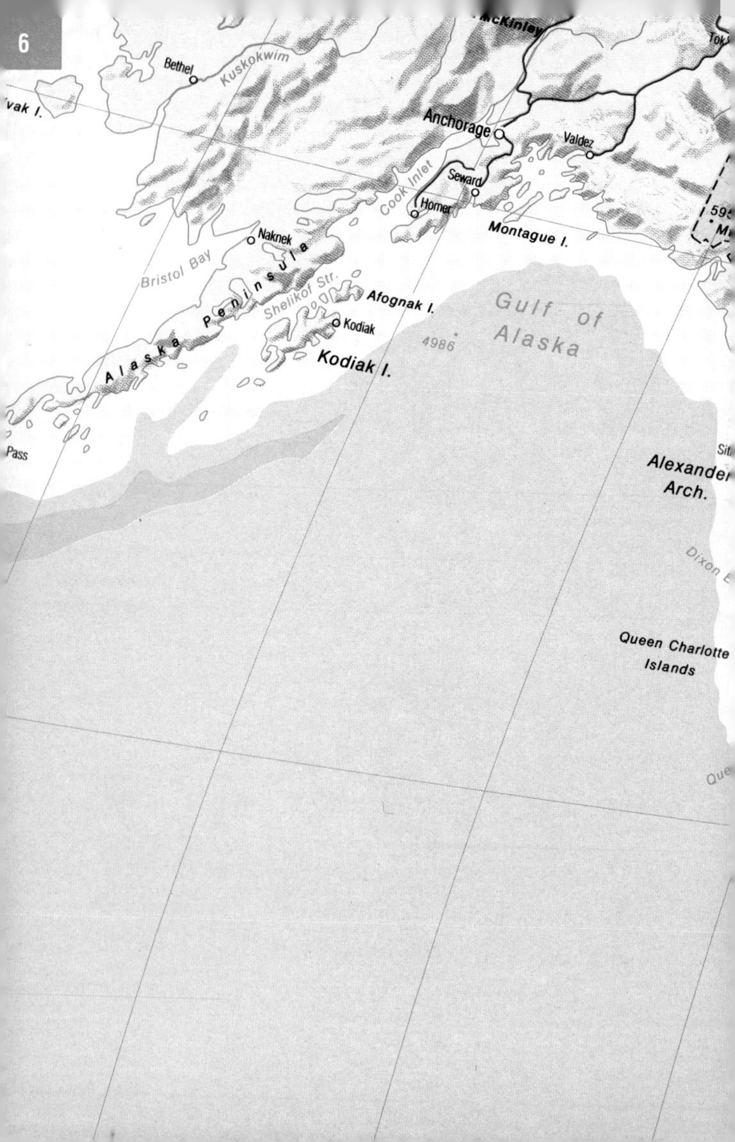

McKinley
Bethel
Kuskokwim
Anchorage
Valdez
Seward
Cook Inlet
Homer
Naknek
Montague I.
Bristol Bay
Alaska Peninsula
Shelikof Str.
Afognak I.
Kodiak
Kodiak I.
Gulf of Alaska
4986
Pass
Alexander Arch.
Queen Charlotte Islands

TERRITORY
Dawson
Mayo
Yukon
Whitehorse
Watson Lake
Fort Simpson
Fort Providence
Yellowknife
Great Slave Lake
Hay River
Fort Smith
Uranium
Fort Nelson
High Level
Peace R.
L. Athabasca
Athabasca
Fort McMurray
La Loche
La Ronge
Coast Mountains
Stewart
Prince Rupert
BRITISH COLUMBIA
ROCKY MOUNTAINS
Dawson Creek
Valleyview
ALBERTA
SASKATCHEWAN
Prince George
Bella Coola
Mt. Robson 3954
Jasper
Edmonton
Prince Albert
North Battleford
Saskatoon
Kamloops
Revelstoke
Banff
Calgary
Vancouver
Vancouver I.
Victoria
Kelowna
Lethbridge
Medicine Hat
Moose Jaw
Regina
WASHINGTON
Tacoma
Seattle
Olympia
4390 Mt. Rainier
Spokane
Havre
Great Falls
Missouri
Glendive
Helena
MONTANA
Columbia
Portland
Salem
Butte
Bozeman
Billings
Bismarck
OREGON
IDAHO
Yellowstone
SOUTH DAK
NORTH DA
NORTH

Chesterfield Inlet
Fort Smith
Eskimo Point
257
Uranium City
L. Athabasca
C A N A D A
Churchill
Reindeer Lake
Lynn Lake
Nelson
Thompson
La Ronge
MANITOBA
SASKATCHEWAN
Flin Flon
Fort Severn
Prince Albert
Saskatchewan
Grand Rapids
Saskatoon
L. Winnipeg
Yorkton
Regina
Pickle Lake
Moosonee
Winnipeg
Kenora
ONTARIO
Brandon
L. Nipigon
L. of the Woods
Nipigon
Minot
Fort Frances
Cochrane
Thunder Bay
NORTH DAKOTA
Timmins
L. Superior
Bismarck
Fargo
Duluth
Sault Ste Marie
Sudbury
MINNESOTA
MICHIGAN
Escanaba
North Bay
SOUTH DAKOTA
St. Paul
Green Bay
Parry Sound
Pierre
Minneapolis
WISCONSIN
Rapid City
Sioux Falls
Mississippi
L. Huron
Kingston
La Crosse
L. Michigan
Missouri
Milwaukee
Grand Rapids
Toronto
Sioux City
Flint
L. Ontario
NEBRASKA
Madison
Rochester
IOWA
Lansing
Niagara Falls
North Platte
Omaha
Chicago
London
Buffalo
Davenport
Detroit
Lincoln
L. Erie
Erie
Des Moines
Gary
Toledo
Cleveland
Scranton
Platte
Peoria
UNITED STATES
Akron
PENNSYLVANIA
ILLINOIS
INDIANA
OHIO
Harrisburg
Dayton
Pittsburgh
Topeka
Missouri
Springfield
Philadelphia
Columbus
Dodge City
KANSAS
Kansas City
St. Louis
Indianapolis
Cincinnati
Baltimore
Ohio
Jefferson City
Washington
Wichita
Frankfort
W. VIRGINIA
Annapolis

C. Mercy
Salisbury I.
Iqaluit
Nottingham I.
Mansel I.
Hudson Str.
Resolution I.
Labrador Sea
Akpatok I.
C. Chidley
Povungnituk
Ungava Bay
3240
Inukjuak
Kuujjuaq
Hebron
Labrador
Nain
Poste-de-la-Baleine
NEWFOUNDLAND
Schefferville
Michikamau L.
Cartwright
Labrador City
Goose Bay
QUEBEC
Réservoir Manicouagan
St. Anthony
L. Mistassini
Chibougamau
Sept-Iles
Havre-St-Pierre
Harrington-Harbour
Baie-Comeau
Anticosti I.
L. St-Jean
Island of Newfoundland
Corner Brook
Gaspé
Chicoutimi
G. of St. Lawrence
Gander
Channel-Port aux Basques
Québec
NEW BRUNSWICK
PRINCE EDWARD I.
Cape Breton I.
St. John's
Houlton
Fredericton
Charlottetown
Sydney
St-Pierre-et-Miquelon
(FR.)
Sherbrooke
MAINE
Moncton
Louisbourg
St. John
NOVA SCOTIA
Augusta
1917
Halifax
Yarmouth
VT.
N.H.
Portland
Concord
Sable I. (CAN.)
Boston
C. Cod
Providence
New Haven
New York

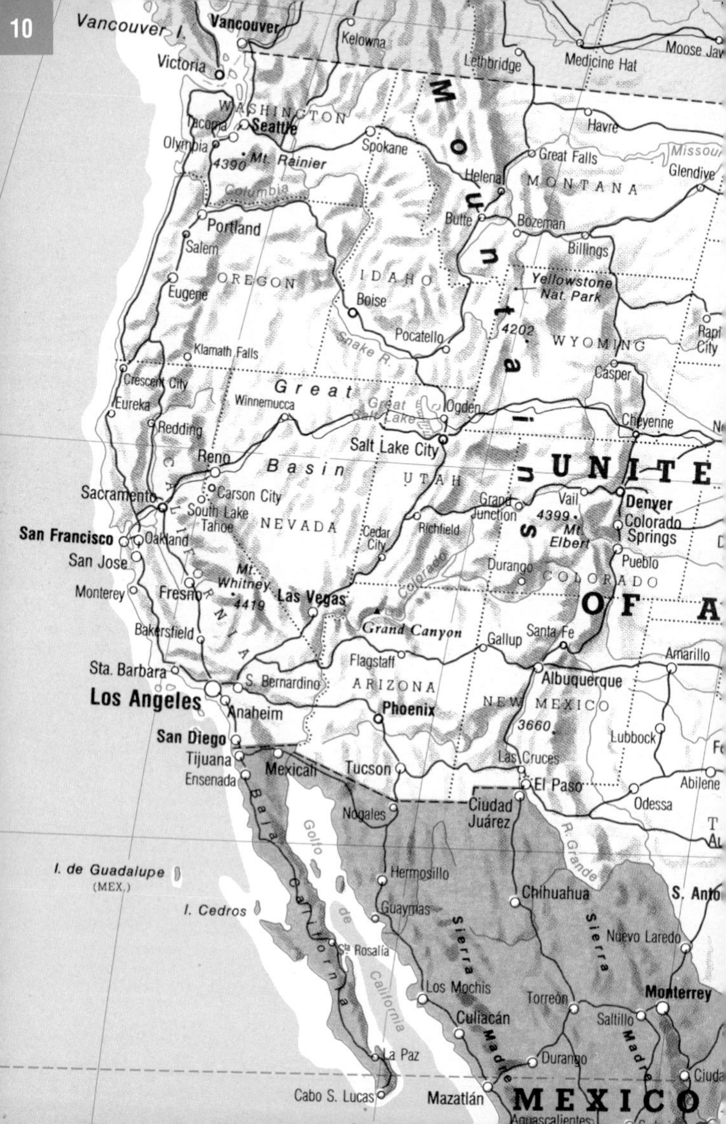
Vancouver I.
Vancouver
Victoria
Kelowna
Lethbridge
Medicine Hat
Moose Jaw
WASHINGTON
Tacoma
Seattle
Olympia
Spokane
4390 Mt. Rainier
Columbia
Havre
Great Falls
Missouri
Glendive
Helena
MONTANA
Butte
Bozeman
Billings
Portland
Salem
Eugene
OREGON
IDAHO
Boise
Pocatello
Snake R.
Yellowstone Nat. Park
4202
WYOMING
Rapid City
Casper
Klamath Falls
Crescent City
Eureka
Redding
Great Basin
Winnemucca
Great Salt Lake
Ogden
Salt Lake City
Cheyenne
UNITED STATES OF AMERICA
Mountains
Reno
Carson City
Sacramento
South Lake Tahoe
NEVADA
UTAH
Grand Junction
Vail
Denver
4399 Mt. Elbert
Colorado Springs
Pueblo
San Francisco
Oakland
San Jose
Monterey
Fresno
Cedar City
Richfield
Colorado
Durango
COLORADO
CALIFORNIA
Mt. Whitney 4419
Las Vegas
Grand Canyon
Bakersfield
Gallup
Santa Fe
Amarillo
Sta. Barbara
Flagstaff
ARIZONA
Los Angeles
S. Bernardino
Albuquerque
NEW MEXICO
Anaheim
Phoenix
3660
San Diego
Lubbock
Tijuana
Mexicali
Tucson
Las Cruces
Ensenada
El Paso
Abilene
Odessa
Ciudad Juárez
Nogales
Baja California
Golfo de California
R. Grande
I. de Guadalupe (MEX.)
Hermosillo
Chihuahua
S. Antonio
I. Cedros
Guaymas
Sierra Madre
Nuevo Laredo
Sta Rosalía
Los Mochis
Torreón
Monterrey
Culiacán
Saltillo
La Paz
Durango
Cabo S. Lucas
Mazatlán
MEXICO
Aguascalientes

Pickle Lake
Bay
Moosonee
Winnipeg
Kenora
ONTARIO
Brandon
L. of the Woods
L. Nipigon
Chibou
Minot
Fort Frances
Nipigon
Cochrane
Matagami
Thunder Bay
DAKOTA
Timmins
L. Superior
Fargo
Duluth
Sault Ste Marie
Sudbury
MINNESOTA
MICHIGAN
Escanaba
DAKOTA
North Bay
St. Paul
Green Bay
Parry Sound
Minneapolis
WISCONSIN
L. Michigan
L. Huron
Ottawa
Mississippi
Sioux Falls
La Crosse
Kingston
Missouri
Toronto
Grand Rapids
Milwaukee
Flint
L. Ontario
Sioux City
Madison
Niagara Falls
Rochester
Syracuse
IOWA
Lansing
Albany
Chicago
London
Omaha
Davenport
Detroit
Buffalo
NEW YORK
Lincoln
Des Moines
L. Erie
Erie
Toledo
Cleveland
Scranton
Hartford
Peoria
Gary
STATES
Akron
PENNSYLVANIA
ILLINOIS
INDIANA
OHIO
Harrisburg
Newark
Dayton
Pittsburgh
Topeka
Springfield
Missouri
Philadelphia
Trenton
Columbus
Indianapolis
Kansas City
St. Louis
Cincinnati
Baltimore
N.J.
Atlantic Ci
Jefferson City
Ohio
Washington
Dover
Frankfort
W. VIRGINIA
Annapolis
DE.
Evansville
Springfield
MISSOURI
Louisville
Charleston
MD.
Richmond
ERICA
Williamsburg
KENTUCKY
Roanoke
VIRGINIA
Newport News
Tulsa
Nashville
Knoxville
Norfolk
Appalachian Mts.
2037
Greensboro
City
TENNESSEE
Raleigh
ARKANSAS
Memphis
NORTH
C. Hatteras
Charlotte
Huntsville
Chattanooga
Little Rock
CAROLINA
Columbia
Mississippi
Birmingham
Atlanta
Wilmington
MISSISSIPPI
SOUTH CAROLINA
Myrtle Beach
Macon
Dallas
Jackson
ALABAMA
Charleston
Shreveport
Columbus
Natchez
Montgomery
Savannah
GEORGIA
Mobile
Baton Rouge
Beaumont
Pensacola
Jacksonville
LOUISIANA
Tallahassee
New Orleans
St. Augustine
Galveston
Daytona Beach
FLORIDA
Tampa
C. Canaveral
Orlando
Gulf of Mexico
St. Petersburg
West Palm Beach
Grd. Bahama
BAHAMAS
Fort Lauderdale
Abaco
Miami
Nassau
Eleuthera
Key West
Cat I.
Andros I.
Str. of Florida
Long I.
Havana
Santa Clara

MEXICO
Mexico
Guadalajara
Monterrey
Chihuahua
Gulf of Mexico
Bahía de Campeche
Yucatán
GUATEMALA
BELIZE
HONDURAS
EL SALVADOR
NICARAGUA
COSTA RICA
Havana
Dallas
Houston
S. Antonio
New Orleans
Galápagos Islands
(Arch. de Colón)
(ECUADOR)
Islas Revilla Gigedo (MEX.)
I. del Coco
(C.R.)
I. de Malpelo
(COL.)

Bermuda Is.
Hamilton
(U.K.)
Charleston
Savannah
SARGASSO S
Grd. Bahama
BAHAMAS
Abaco
Nassau
Eleuthera
Cat I.
Long I.
Acklins I.
Inagua
Turks and Caicos Is.
(U.K.)
Cockburn Town
Holguín
Santiago de Cuba
DOMINICAN REP.
HAITI
Santiago
Port-au-Prince
Sto. Domingo
Kingston
Puerto Rico
(U.S.A.)
S. Juan
Virgin Is. (U.S.A.)
Virgin Is. (U.K.)
Anguilla (U.K.)
Ned. Antillen (NETH.)
St-Barthélemy (FR.)
ANTIGUA AND BARBUDA
St. John's
Basseterre
ST. CHRISTOPHER AND NEVIS
Pointe-à-Pitre
Guadeloupe (FR.)
Montserrat (U.K.)
Roseau
DOMINICA
Fort-de-France
Martinique (FR.)
Castries
SAINT LUCIA
ST. VINCENT AND THE GRENADINES
Kingstown
Bridgetown
BARBADOS
St George's
GRENADA
ANTILLES
Antilles
Caribbean Sea
Lesser Antilles
5058
4603
8962
Willemstad
Curaçao (NETH.)
Margarita
Tobago
TRINIDAD AND TOBAGO
Port of Spain
Trinidad
Barranquilla
Cartagena
Maracaibo
L. de Maracaibo
5835
Coro
Caracas
Cumaná
Barquisimeto
Valencia
Barcelona
Montería
Mérida
Cúcuta
San Cristóbal
Orinoco
Ciudad Guayana
Ciudad Bolivar
VENEZUELA
Bucaramanga
Magdalena
Georgetown
New Amsterdam
GUYANA
Paramaribo
SURINAME
2800
Medellín
Manizales
Ibagué
Bogotá
Cali
5800
Popayán
Neiva
COLOMBIA
Guaviare
Esmeralda
Boa Vista
RORAIMA
Branco
Pasto
R. Negro
Japurá
Óbidos
Amazonia
Chimborazo

THE GRENADINES
Bridgetown
Kingstown
St George's
GRENADA
Curaçao (NETH.)
Willemstad
Margarita
Tobago
TRINIDAD
Port of Spain
Trinidad
Caracas
Cumaná
Barranquilla
Cartagena
Maracaibo
Coro
L. de Maracaibo
5835
Barquisimeto
Valencia
Barcelona
Colón
Panama
Pto Limón
David
PANAMA
La Palma
Panama Canal
Montería
Mérida
Cúcuta
San Cristóbal
Ciudad Guayana
Ciudad Bolivar
Orinoco
Bucaramanga
Magdalena
VENEZUELA
Medellín
Manizales
GUYANA
2800
Buenaventura
Ibagué
Bogotá
Malpelo (COL.)
Cali
5800
Guaviare
Esmeralda
Boa Vista
Popayán
Neiva
COLOMBIA
Pasto
Branco
RORAIMA
Quito
ECUADOR
6267
Chimborazo
Riobamba
Guayaquil
Cuenca
R. Negro
Japurá
Manaus
Amazon
Napo
Iquitos
Fonte Boa
Solimões
Marañón
Piura
AMAZONAS
Ucayali
Juruá
Madeira
Chiclayo
Cajamarca
Purus
Humaitá
Cruzeiro do Sul
Trujillo
Huascarán
6768
Pucallpa
ACRE
Porto Velho
PERU
Rio Branco
Riberalta
RONDÔNIA
Guaporé
Juruena
Callao
Lima
Huancayo
Pto Maldonado
Machu Picchu
Cuzco
Cordillera de los Andes
Nazca
Beni
BOLIVIA
Puno
L. Titicaca
La Paz
Illimani
6882
Arequipa
Cochabamba
Cáceres
Tacna
Oruro
Santa Cruz
Arica
L. Poopó
Sucre
Potosí
Iquique
Peru-Chile Trench
Mariscal Estigarribia
La Quiaca
Jujuy
8069
Concepción

GO
Kourou
Cayenne
GUYANE (FR.)
AMAPÁ
Macapá
Amazon
Belém
Santarém
Tocantins
Xingu
São Luís
Parnaíba
Fortaleza
Fernando de N (BR.)
MARANHÃO
CEARÁ
RIO GRANDE DO NORTE
Imperatriz
Teresina
Quixadá
Mossoró
C. de São Roque
Natal
Tocantinópolis
Estreito
Juazeiro do Norte
João Pessoa
Picos
PARAÍBA
Campina Grande
Recife
PIAUÍ
PERNAMBUCO
Miracema do Tocantins
Paulo Afonso
Maceió
Araguaia
Juazeiro
ALAGOAS
TOCANTINS
SERGIPE
Aracaju
AZIL
Feira de Santana
GROSSO
Salvador
BAHIA
São Francisco
GOIÁS
Vitória da Conquista
Ilhéus
Brasília
Goiás
Montes Claros
Goiânia
Pirapora
Teófilo Otoni
Caravelas
MINAS GERAIS
Uberlândia
ESPÍRITO SANTO
ATO GROSSO
Uberaba
Belo Horizonte
Vitória
Trindad (BR.)
São José do Rio Preto
Ribeirão Preto
Ouro Preto
2890
Grande
DO SUL
Paraná
SÃO PAULO
Juiz de Fora
Campos
C. de São Tomé
Nova Iguaçu
RIO DE JANEIRO
Bauru
Niterói
Londrina
Campinas
Maringá
Rio de Janeiro

BOLIVIA
Nazca
Puno
L. Titicaca
La Paz
Illimani
6882
Arequipa
Cochabamba
Tacna
Oruro
Santa Cruz
L. Poopó
Arica
Sucre
Potosí
Iquique
Cáceres
Peru-Chile Trench
Mariscal Estigarribia
Paraguay
La Quiaca
JUJUY
8069
Concepci
PAR
Antofagasta
S. Salvador de J.
Pilcomayo
Teuco
Salta
FORMOSA
Formos
Islas Desventuradas
(CH.)
SALTA
S. Miguel de Tucumán
CHACO
Resistencia
6863
CATAMARCA
Copiapó
TUC.
Santiago del Estero
Catamarca
SANTIAGO DEL ESTERO
Salado
LA RIOJA
La Rioja
Paraná
La Serena
SANTA FE
CÓRDOBA
SAN JUAN
San Juan
Concor
Córdoba
Santa Fe
Paraná
Villa María
Aconcagua 6960
Mendoza
Río Cuarto
ENTRE RÍOS
Valparaiso
Rosario
I. R. Crusoe
Santiago
San Luis
Islas Juan Fernández
(CH.)
Rancagua
San Rafael
SAN LUIS
Buenos Aires
Pehuajó
Talca
MENDOZA
Chillán
Santa Rosa
BUENOS
Salado
Olavarría
Concepción
Colorado
Tand
LA PAMPA
Bahía Blanca
NEUQUÉN
Neuquén
Temuco
R. Negro
Río Colorado
Bahía
Valdivia
RÍO NEGRO
S. Antonio Oeste
Viedma
Puerto Montt
S. Carlos de Bariloche
G. San Matías
Pen. Valdés
I. de Chiloé
CHUBUT
Chubut
Esquel
Rawson
Arch. de los Chonos
Puerto Aisén
Comodoro Rivadavia
G. San Jorge
4058
Perito Moreno
CHILE
ARGENTINA
Ande de Ande

Brasília
Goiás
Goiânia
Conquista
Ilhéus
Montes Claros
Pirapora
Teófilo Otoni
Caravelas
MINAS GERAIS
ESPÍRITO SANTO
Uberlândia
Uberaba
GROSSO
Belo Horizonte
Vitória
Trindade
(BR.)
São José do Rio Preto
Ribeirão Preto
Ouro Preto
2890
DO SUL
SÃO PAULO
Juiz de Fora
Campos
C. de São Tomé
Bauru
Nova Iguaçu
RIO DE JANEIRO
Londrina
Campinas
Niterói
Maringá
São Paulo
Rio de Janeiro
PARANA
Santos
Foz do Iguaçu
Guarapuava
Ponta Grossa
Curitiba
Iguaçú Falls
Joinville
STA CATARINA
MISIONES
Lajes
Florianópolis
Passo Fundo
RIO GRANDE DO SUL
Caxias do Sul
Santa Maria
Porto Alegre
Bagé
Pelotas
Rio Grande
GUAY
La Paloma
Punta del Este
de la Plata
C. San Antonio
Pinamar
Mar del Plata
S
5845

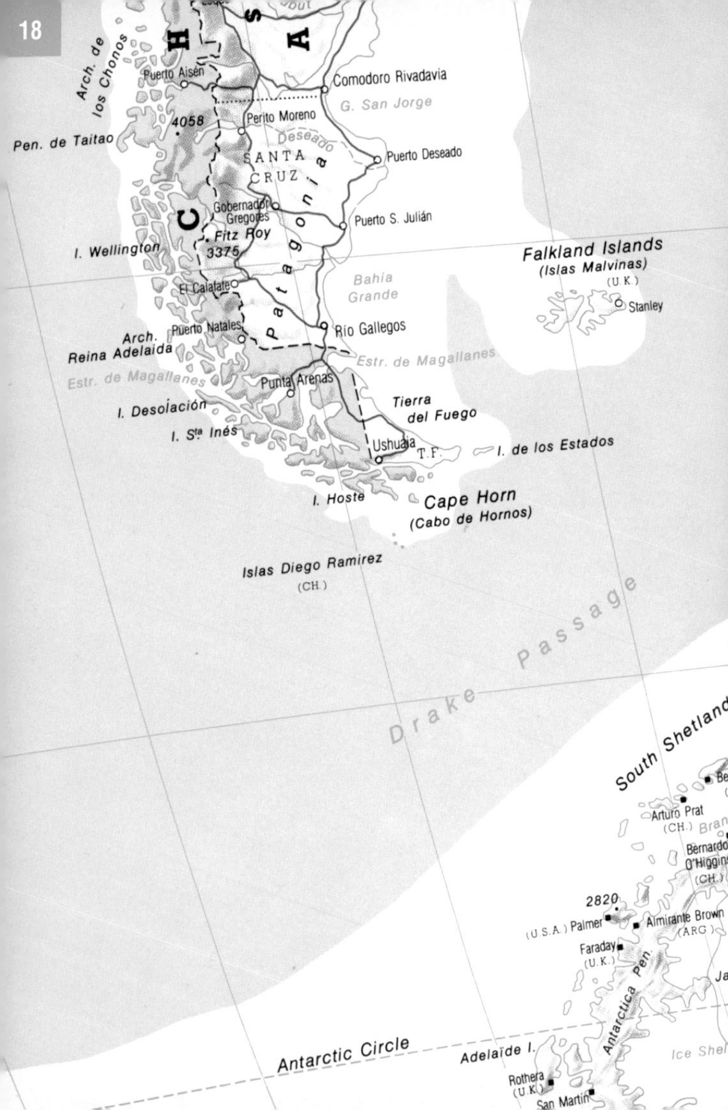
Arch. de los Chonos
Puerto Aisén
Comodoro Rivadavia
G. San Jorge
4058
Perito Moreno
Pen. de Taitao
Deseado
SANTA CRUZ
Puerto Deseado
Patagonia
Gobernador Gregores
Puerto S. Julián
Fitz Roy 3375
I. Wellington
Falkland Islands
(Islas Malvinas)
(U.K.)
Stanley
Bahia Grande
El Calafate
Arch. Reina Adelaida
Puerto Natales
Río Gallegos
Estr. de Magallanes
Estr. de Magallanes
Punta Arenas
I. Desolación
Tierra del Fuego
I. Sta Inés
Ushuaia
T.F.
I. de los Estados
I. Hoste
Cape Horn
(Cabo de Hornos)
Islas Diego Ramirez
(CH.)
Drake Passage
South Shetland
Arturo Prat
(CH.)
Bernardo O'Higgins
(CH.)
2820
(U.S.A.) Palmer
Almirante Brown
(ARG.)
Faraday
(U.K.)
Antarctica Pen.
Antarctic Circle
Adelaide I.
Rothera
(U.K.)
San Martín

South Georgia
(U.K.)
2934

South Sandwich Group (U.K.)
Zavodovski I.
Candlemas Is.
Saunders I.
Montagu I.
Thule Is.

SCOTIA SEA

South Orkney Is.
Signy
(U.K.)
Orcadas (ARG.)

ohant I.
Clarence I.
orge I.
trait
anza (ARG.)
es Ross I.
Marambio (ARG.)

WEDDELL SEA

C. Aldrich
Lincoln Sea
ISLAND
Alert
Nares Strait
Sverdrup Ø
Victoria Fiord
Kap Morris Jesup
1920
Independence Fj.
Knud Rasmussen Land
(Thule)
2150
2100
Hovgaards Ø
Kong Frederik VIII Land
Norske Øer
2050
Melville Bugt
GREENLAND
(Grønland)
x Land
Store Koldewey Ø
Shannon Ø
Upernavik

Disko
Uummannaq
3200
Kong Chri
Traill Ø
Qeqertarsuaq
(Godhavn)
Ilulissat (Jakobshavn)
Aasiaat
(Egedesminde)
Qasigiannguit (Christianshåb)
Ittoqqortoormiit
(Scoresbysund)
Kap Brewster
Gunnbjørns Fjeld
3700
Kangerlussuaq
(Sdr. Strømfjord)
Mont Forel
3360
Denmark Strait
Ammassalik
Isafjördur
Akureyri
Seydisfjördur
ICELAND
Reykjavík
2119
Nuuk
Kong Frederik VI Kyst
Paamiut
(Frederikshåb)
Narsarsuaq
Qaqortoq (Julianehåb)
Nanortalik
Kap Farvel
Rockall (U.K.)

St. Anthony

rbour

Island of Newfoundland

er Brook

Gander

Basques

St. John's

S!-Pierre-et-Miquelon

(FR.)

AN.)

NORT

ATLANT

OCEAN

I. Flore

I.

(Arquipéla

E A

Tropic of Cancer

Stranraer
Belfast
Galway
Dublin
IRELAND
Cork
Liverpool
Manchester
Birmingham
Cardiff
Plymouth
Southampton
English Chann
Le Hav
Brest
Rennes
Nantes
Bay of
Biscay
Bordeau
La Coruña
Bilbao
Biarritz
C. Finisterre
5354
Oviedo
S. Sebastian
Vigo
Valladolid
Zaragoza
Porto
SPAIN
Madrid
Coimbra
PORTUGAL
R. Tajo
Valencia
Lisbon
Badajoz
Córdoba
Sevilla
Granada
Cádiz
Gibraltar (U.K.)
Strait of Gibraltar
Tanger
Ceuta (SP.)
Melilla (SP.)
Rabat (Ar Ribat)
Fès
Oujda
Tlemcen
Casablanca (Dar el Beïda)
Meknès
MOROCCO (AL MAGHRIB)
Safi
Marrakech
Béchar
4167
J. Toubkal
Ouarzazate
Agadir
Hamada du Drâa
O. Draa
Tindouf
Reggane
Tanezrou
I. Terceira
I. São Miguel
Açores)
Funchal
Madeira Islands (PORT.)
La Palma
Lanzarote
Tenerife
Las Palmas
Santa Cruz de Tenerife
Fuerteventura
Gran Canaria
Tarfaya
Laâyoune
Canary Islands (Islas Canarias) (SPAIN)
Sahara
Dakhla

(SPAIN)
Cancer
Tanez
Western Sahar
Dakhla
Zouérat
Nouâdhibou
Atâr
MAURITANIA
MA
S
S
Nouakchott
Tombouctou
Néma
Kiffa
Sénégal
St-Louis
SENEGAL
Santo Antão
Boa Vista
São Tiago
CAPE VERDE
Praia
C. Vert
Dakar
Kaolack
Kayes
Ségou
Niger
Ouahigo
Ouaga
5350
GAMBIA
Banjul
Tambacounda
Bamako
Bissau
GUINEA-BISSAU
Labe
GUINEA
Fouta Djalon
Mamou
BURKINA
Bobo-Dioulasso
Tamale
Conakry
Kankan
1945
Loma Mts.
Korhogo
Freetown
SIERRA
LEONE
Bo
Nzérékoré
IVORY
COAST
Bouaké
Daloa
Yamoussoukro
GH
Kuma
Monrovia
LIBERIA
Abidjan
Accra
Harper
San-Pédro
Sekondi-
Penedos de
of

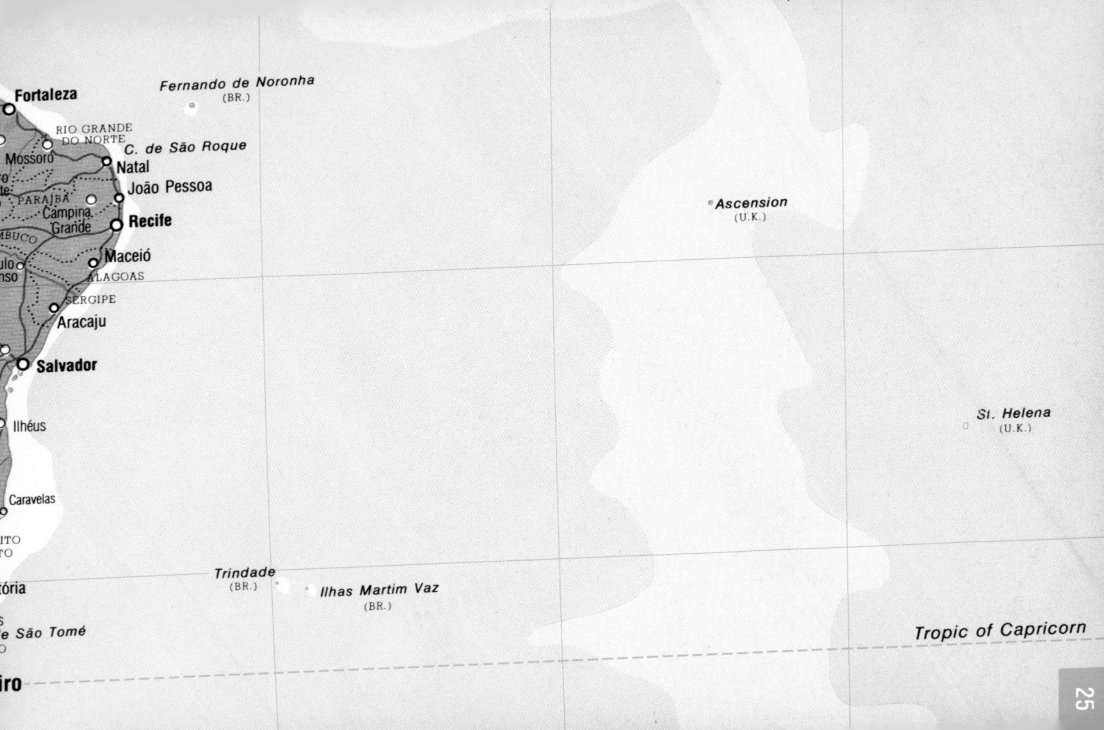
Fortaleza
Fernando de Noronha
(BR.)
RIO GRANDE
DO NORTE
Mossoró
C. de São Roque
Natal
João Pessoa
PARAÍBA
Campina
Grande
Recife
Maceió
ALAGOAS
SERGIPE
Aracaju
Salvador
Ilhéus
Caravelas
Ascension
(U.K.)
St. Helena
(U.K.)
Trindade
(BR.)
Ilhas Martim Vaz
(BR.)
de São Tomé
Tropic of Capricorn

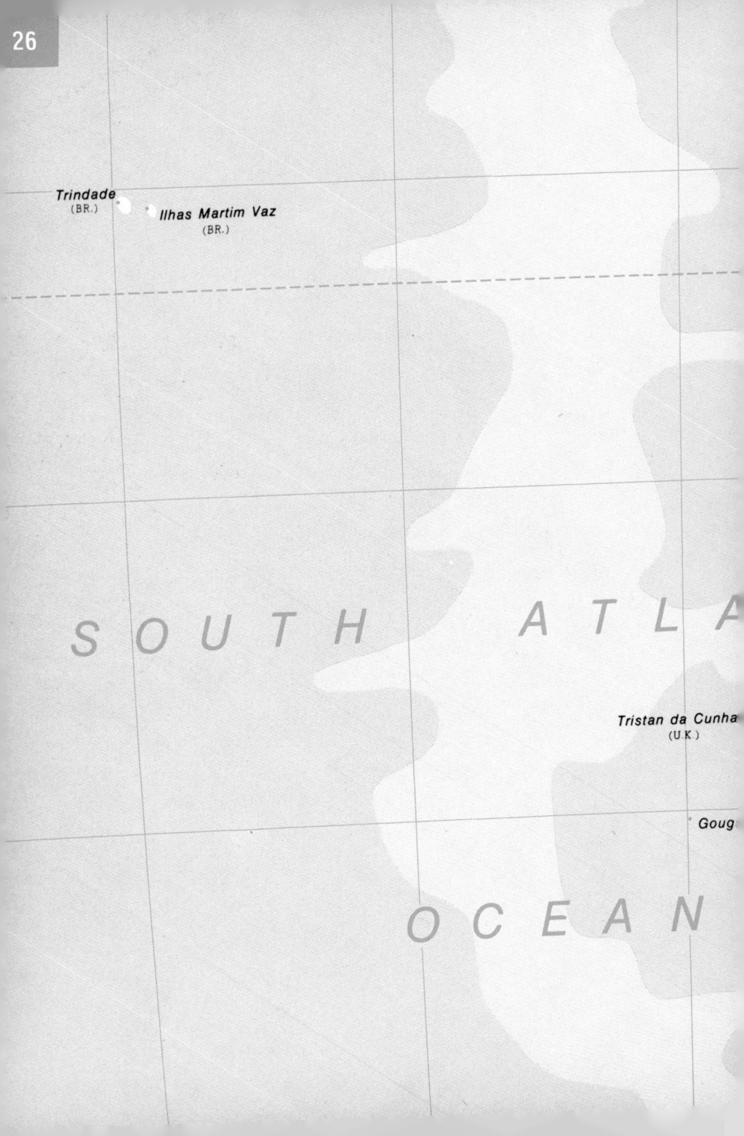

Trindade
(BR.)
Ilhas Martim Vaz
(BR.)

SOUTH ATLA

Tristan da Cunha
(U.K.)

Goug

OCEAN

5752
St. Helena
(U.K.)
Namibe
Tsumeb
NAMIBIA
2579
Windhoek
Gobabis
Walvisbaai
(S.A.)
of Capricorn
Keetmanshoop
Lüderitz
Orange
Springbok
Malmesbury
Cape Town
Cape of Good Hope
TIC

ARCTIC O
ordostrundingen
Spitsbergen
Nordaustlandet
Kong Ka
Land
Vestspitsbergen
1712
Longyearbyen
Edgeøya
Svalbard
(NORWAY)
Bjørnøya
N
Hammerfest
NORWEGIAN
n Mayen
(NOR.)
Tromsø
SEA
Vesterålen
Narvik
NORWAY
Kiruna
Lofoten
2111
Lap
Bodø
Malmberget
Arctic Circle
3312
Mo i Rana
Dønna
Luleå

E A N
O. Rudol'fa
O-va Belaja Zeml'a
O. Greem-Bell
O. Zeml'a Aleksandry
O. Sal'm
O. Zeml'a Georga
tøya
Franz Josef Land
(Zeml'a Franca-Iosifa)
BARENTS SEA
Novaja Zeml'a
1590
162
pr. Karskije Vorota
O. Vaj
Pečorskoje More
O. Kolgujev
Kirkenes
Zapol'arnyj
Murmansk
Češskaja Guba
Narjan-Mar
Kolskij Poluostrov
Pečora
Kirovsk
More
Kuzomen'
Beloje (White Sea)
Mezen'
Pečora
Kalevala
Archangel'sk

Ittoqqortoormiit
(Scoresbysund)
Kap Brewster
Jan Mayen
(NOR.)
NORWEG
SEA
Strait
Arctic Circle
3312
Isafjördur
Akureyri
Seydisfjördur
ICELAND
Reykjavík
2119
Færøerne
(DEN.)
(U.K.)
Shetland Is.
Orkney Is.
Thurso
Hebrides
Rockall (U.K.)
110
Inverness
Aberdeen
Dundee
Glasgow
Edinburgh
UNITED KINGDOM
Londonderry
Stranraer
Newcastle
Belfast
Leeds
Galway
Dublin
Liverpool
Sheffield
Manchester
Norwich
IRELAND
Birmingham
Den Haag
London
Rotterdam
Cork
Cardiff
Antwerpen
Dover
Calais
Plymouth
Southampton
Lille
English Channel
Rouen
Paris
Le Havre
Brest
Rennes
Le Mans
Loire
Tours
Nantes
FRANCE
Stavang

(Nordkapp)
Hammerfest
Kirkenes
Tromsø
Inari
Zapol'arnyj
Murmansk
Ivalo
Vesterålen
Narvik
NORWAY
Kolskij
Poluostrov
Kiruna
Lofoten
Lapland
Kirovsk
2111
Malmberget
Bodø
Kuzomen'
Rovaniemi
Mo i Rana
Beloje
Kuusamo
Dønna
Kalevala
Luleå
Kem'
Oulu
Severodvinsk
SWEDEN
Gulf of Bothnia
FINLAND
Umeå
Medvežjegorsk
Trondheim
Vaasa
Joensuu
Östersund
Kuopio
Petrozavodsk
Sundsvall
Onežskoje Oz
Tampere
Mora
Ladožskoje Ozero
Lodejnoje Pole
Turku
Kotka
Vyborg
Helsinki
G. of Finland
Oslo
Uppsala
Čerepove
Leningrad
Stockholm
Tallinn
Örebro
Vänern
ESTONIA
Novgorod
Rybinsk
Čudskoje Ozero
Norrköping
Pärnu
Vättern
Gotland
Saaremaa
Baltic Sea
Pskov
Göteborg
Kalinin
Jönkoping
LATVIA
Daugava
Ålborg
Rīga
Velikije Luki
Karlskrona
Öland
Daugavpils
DENMARK
Klaipėda
Moscow
(Moskva)
Copenhagen
LITHUANIA
Malmö
Kaunas
Odense
Kaliningrad
Vitebsk
Smolensk
Kaluga
Bornholm
Gdynia
Vilnius
Kiel
Minsk
Rostock
Gdańsk
Lübeck
Mogil'ov
Br'ansk
Grodno
Szczecin
Białystok
Dnepr
BYELORUSSIA
Berlin
POLAND
Warsaw
Gomel'
Hannover
Brest
Pinsk
Poznań
Łódź
Černigov
GERMANY
Lublin
Sumy
Wrocław
Wisła
Dresden
Rovno
Leipzig
Częstochowa
Kiev (Kijev)
Frankfurt
Prague
Gliwice
Katowice
Žitomir
Poltava
Plzeň
Ostrava
L'vov
UKRAINE
Nürnberg
Kraków
Dnestr
CZECHOSLOVAKIA
Košice
Vinnica
Čerkassy
Stuttgart
Regensburg
Vienna
Carpathian
Bratislava
Černovcy
München
Salzburg
Krivoj Rog
Miskolc
Zürich
AUSTRIA
MOLDAVIA
Kišin'ov
Budapest
Innsbruck
Cherson
Graz
Cluj-Napoca
Iaşi
Melitopol
LIECH.
HUNGARY
Ljubljana
Odessa

FINLAND
Vaasa
Kuopio
Joensuu
Tampere
Turku
Helsinki
Kotka
Vyborg
G. of Finland
Severodvinsk
Usogorsk
Medvežjegorsk
Bereznik
Sev. Dvina
Petrozavodsk
Onežskoje Oz.
Kargopol'
Kotlas
Ladožskoje Ozero
Lodejnoje Pole
Leningrad
Čerepovec
Vologda
Tallinn
ESTONIA
Čudskoje Ozero
Novgorod
Rybinskoje Vdchr.
Šarja
Rybinsk
Kostroma
Pärnu
Saaremaa
Pskov
Jaroslavl'
Ivanovo
Kalinin
Volga
LATVIA
Rīga
Daugava
Velikije Luki
Zagorsk
Vladimir
Čeboksary
Moscow
(Moskva)
Orechovo-Zujevo
Daugavpils
Klaipėda
LITHUANIA
Kaunas
Kolomna
Podol'sk
Oka
Saransk
R'azan'
Kaliningrad
Vitebsk
Smolensk
Kaluga
Tula
Vilnius
Minsk
Mogil'ov
Br'ansk
Dnepr
Grodno
Lipeck
Tambov
Penza
Białystok
Or'ol
BYELORUSSIA
Warsaw
Wisła
Brest
Pinsk
Gomel'
Kursk
Voronež
Černigov
Sumy
Łódź
Lublin
Kamyšin
Częstochowa
Rovno
Kiev (Kijev)
Char'kov
Don
Katowice
Žitomir
Poltava
Kraków
L'vov
UKRAINE
Dnestr
Dnepropetrovsk
Vorošilovgrad
Košice
Vinnica
Čerkassy
Doneck
Šachty
Bratislava
Miskolc
Černovcy
Carpathians
MOLDAVIA
Krivoj Rog
Zaporožje
Rostov-na-Donu
Budapest
Kišin'ov
Cherson
Mariupol'
HUNGARY
Cluj-Napoca
Iaşi
Melitopol'
Azovskoje More
Odessa
Timişoara
Braşov
Galaţi
Kerč'
Stavropol'
Belgrade
ROMANIA
Bucharest
Sevastopol'
1545
Krasnodar
Craiova
Constanţa
Jalta
Gora El'brus
5633
GOSLAVIA
Danube
Ruse
Soči
Black Sea
Sarajevo
Varna
Suchumi
BULGARIA
Kutaisi
Dubrovnik
Sofia
Plovdiv
Burgas
2245
Titograd
Batumi
GEORGIA
Samsun
Trabzon
Tirane
Skopje
Istanbul
Leninakan
ALBANIA
2917
Thessaloníki
Ankara
Sivas
Olympus
Lárissa
Bursa
Erzurum
5137
Aegean Sea
TURKEY
(TÜRKIYE)
Afyon
Elâzığ
GREECE
(HELLAS)
Kayseri
Van
Izmir
Pátra
Athens
Adana
Gaziantep
Antalya

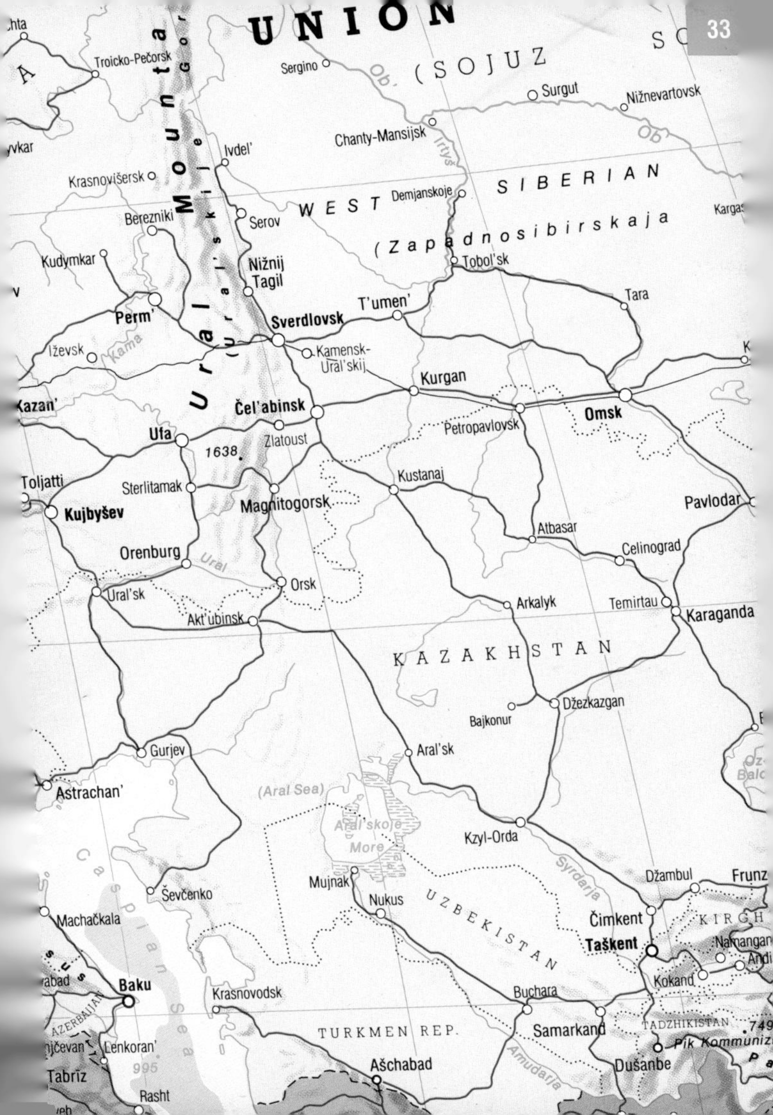
UNION
(SOJUZ
WEST SIBERIAN
(Zapadnosibirskaja
Ural Mountains
(Ural'skije Gory)
KAZAKHSTAN
UZBEKISTAN
TURKMEN REP.
TADZHIKISTAN
AZERBAIJAN
KIRGH
Troicko-Pečorsk
Sergino
Surgut
Nižnevartovsk
Chanty-Mansijsk
Ivdel'
Krasnovišersk
Demjanskoje
Serov
Berezniki
Kudymkar
Tobol'sk
Nižnij Tagil
Tara
Perm'
T'umen'
Sverdlovsk
Iževsk
Kamensk-Ural'skij
Kurgan
Kazan'
Čel'abinsk
Omsk
Petropavlovsk
Ufa
Zlatoust
1638
Toljatti
Sterlitamak
Kustanaj
Kujbyšev
Magnitogorsk
Pavlodar
Atbasar
Orenburg
Celinograd
Orsk
Ural'sk
Arkalyk
Temirtau
Karaganda
Akt'ubinsk
Džezkazgan
Bajkonur
Gurjev
Aral'sk
Astrachan'
(Aral Sea)
Aral'skoje More
Kzyl-Orda
Syrdarja
Mujnak
Džambul
Frunz
Nukus
Ševčenko
Machačkala
Čimkent
Taškent
Namangan
Kokand
Baku
Krasnovodsk
Buchara
Samarkand
Pik Kommunizi
Lenkoran'
Dušanbe
Aščhabad
Amudarja
Tabriz
Rasht
Caspian Sea
995
Kama
Ural
Ob'
Irtyš
Kargas

UNITED KINGDOM
IRELAND
DENMARK
NETH.
BELG.
LUX.
GERMANY
FRANCE
SWITZ.
LIECH.
MONACO
ANDORRA
SPAIN
PORTUGAL
VATICAN CITY
S. MARINO
MOROCCO
(AL MAGHRIB)
TUNISIA
ALGERIA
North Sea
English Channel
Bay of Biscay
Strait of Gibraltar
MEDITERRANEAN
Tyrrhenian Sea
Hebrides
Thurso
Inverness
Aberdeen
Dundee
Glasgow
Edinburgh
Londonderry
Stranraer
Newcastle
Belfast
Leeds
Galway
Dublin
Liverpool
Sheffield
Manchester
Norwich
Birmingham
London
Cork
Cardiff
Dover
Plymouth
Southampton
Stavanger
Kristiansand
Göteborg
Jönköping
Frederikshavn
Ålborg
Karlskrona
Copenhagen
Malmö
Odense
Kiel
Rostock
Lübeck
Hamburg
Groningen
Bremen
Berlin
Hannover
Den Haag
Amsterdam
Rotterdam
Antwerpen
Düsseldorf
Leipzig
Dresden
Köln
Calais
Brussels
Bonn
Frankfurt
Plzeň
Lille
Nürnberg
Rouen
Paris
Le Havre
Nancy
Stuttgart
Regensburg
Brest
Rennes
Le Mans
Strasbourg
München
Salzburg
Loire
Dijon
Basel
Zürich
Innsbruck
Tours
Nantes
Bern
Genève
Lyon
4807
Mt Blanc
Alps
Milano
Venezia
Limoges
Clermont-Fd
Bordeaux
Grenoble
Torino
Genova
Nice
Pisa
Toulouse
Biarritz
Firenze
Montpellier
La Coruña
Bilbao
Pyrénées
Marseille
C. Finisterre
Oviedo
S. Sebastian
Perpignan
Rome
Corse
Ajaccio
Vigo
Valladolid
Zaragoza
Barcelona
Napoli
Porto
Sardegna
Vesuvio
Madrid
Is. Baleares
Menorca
Coimbra
R. Tajo
Palma
Cagliari
Mallorca
Lisbon
Valencia
Ibiza
Badajoz
Palermo
Córdoba
Alicante
Sevilla
Algiers
(el Djazâir)
Bejaïa
Annaba
Bizerte
Sicilia
Granada
Cádiz
Gibraltar (U.K.)
Tunis
Blida
Constantine
Sousse
Oran
Ceuta (SP.)
Melilla (SP.)
Tanger
Saïda
Biskra
Sfax
Gafsa
Rabat
(Ar Ribat)
Fès
Oujda
Tlemcen
Laghouat
I. de Jerba
Gabès
(Tarābulus)
Tripoli
Casablanca
(Dar el Beïda)
Meknès
El-Oued
Ghardaïa
Aïn-Sefra
Ouargla
Safi
Marrakech
Béchar
Hassi-Messaoud
Tripolitania
4167
J. Toubkal
Ouarzazate
Grand Erg occidental
El-Goléa
Grand Erg oriental
Agadir
Ghudāmis
Hamada du Drâa
O. Drâa

Moscow (Moskva)
Novgorod
Rybinsk
Kostroma
Jaroslavl'
Ivanovo
Kalinin
Vladimir
Nižnij Nov
Zagorsk
Čeboksar
Orechovo-Zujevo
Kolomna
Podol'sk
R'azan'
Saransk
Tula
Kaluga
Smolensk
Vitebsk
Velikije Luki
Pskov
Pärnu
Saaremaa
ESTONIA
Čudskoje Ozero
LATVIA
Rīga
Daugava
Daugavpils
Klaipėda
LITHUANIA
Kaunas
Kaliningrad
Vilnius
Minsk
Grodno
Białystok
BYELORUSSIA
Mogil'ov
Br'ansk
Or'ol
Lipeck
Tambov
Penza
Kursk
Voronež
Gomel'
Brest
Pinsk
Černigov
Sumy
Warsaw
Łódź
Lublin
Wisła
Częstochowa
Katowice
Kraków
Rovno
Kiev (Kijev)
Žitomir
Char'kov
Kamyšin
Don
Poltava
L'vov
UKRAINE
Dnepr
Dnestr
Vinnica
Čerkassy
Dnepropetrovsk
Vorošilovgrad
Doneck
Šachty
Košice
Bratislava
Miskolc
Carpathians
Černovcy
MOLDAVIA
Krivoj Rog
Zaporožje
Kišin'ov
Cherson
Mariupol'
Rostov-na-Donu
Budapest
HUNGARY
Cluj-Napoca
Iași
Odessa
Melitopol'
Azovskoje More
Timișoara
Brașov
Galați
Kerč'
Stavropol'
Belgrade
ROMANIA
Bucharest
Sevastopol'
1545
Jalta
Krasnodar
Craiova
Danube
Constanța
Gora El'brus
5633
Soči
Suchumi
Kutaisi
Black Sea
2245
Sarajevo
Ruse
BULGARIA
Varna
Dubrovnik
Titograd
Sofia
Plovdiv
Burgas
Batumi
GEORGIA
Tirane
Skopje
Istanbul
Samsun
Trabzon
Leninakan
ALBANIA
2917
Olympus
Thessaloníki
Ankara
Sivas
Lárissa
Bursa
Erzurum
GREECE (HELLAS)
Aegean Sea
Afyon
TURKEY (TÜRKIYE)
Elâzığ
Kayseri
Van
Pátra
Athens (Athína)
Izmir
Adana
Gaziantep
Antalya
Kikládes
Ionian Sea
Aleppo (Halab)
Dayr az Zawr
Euphrates
5121
Al Lādhiqīyah
Iráklio
Ródos
Nicosia
SYRIA
Homs (Ḥimṣ)
Kríti
CYPRUS
LEBANON
3048
Beirut
Damascus
Haifa
IRAQ
Al Bayḍā'
ISRAEL
Al Maḥallah al Kubrā
Port Said (Būr Sa'īd)
Tel Aviv
Amman
Tubruq
Benghazi (Banghāzī)
Jerusalem
Al Ḥadīthah
Ajdābiyah
Alexandria (Al Iskandarīyah)
Al Ismā'īlīyah
JORDAN
Cyrenaica
(Al Jīzah) Giza
Suez (As Suways)
Pyramids
Al Fayyūm
Cairo
Al 'Aqabah
Sinai
An Nafūd

Sevilla
Granada
Cádiz
Gibraltar (U.K.)
Strait of Gibraltar
Algiers
(el Djazâir)
Blida
Oran
Ceuta
(SP.)
Melilla (SP.)
Tanger
Saïda
Rabat
(Ar Ribat)
Fès
Oujda
Tlemcen
Laghouat
Casablanca
(Dar el Beïda)
Meknès
MOROCCO
(AL MAGHRIB)
Aïn-Sefra
Ghardaïa
Funchal
Madeira Islands
(PORT.)
Safi
Marrakech
Béchar
Grand Erg occidental
El-Goléa
4167
J. Toubkal
Ouarzazate
Agadir
Hamada du Drâa
O. Draa
Lanzarote
La Palma
Tenerife
Las Palmas
Fuerteventura
Gran Canaria
Tarfaya
Tindouf
In Salah
Laâyoune
Reggane
Canary Islands
(Islas Canarias)
(SPAIN)
Western Sahara
Tanezrouft
Dakhla
Tamanghasset
Zouérat
Nouâdhibou
Atâr
MAURITANIA
MALI
Nouakchott
Tombouctou
Néma
Sénégal
Kiffa
Gao
Tahoua
St-Louis
SENEGAL
C. Vert
Dakar
Kaolack
Kayes
Niger
Niamey
Ouahigouya
Ségou
GAMBIA
Banjul
Tambacounda
Bamako
Ouagadougou
Bissau
GUINEA-BISSAU
GUINEA
BURKINA FASO
Kandi
Labé
Fouta Djalon
Bobo-Dioulasso
BENIN
Mamou
Conakry
Kankan
Tamale
Kara
1945
Loma Mts
Korhogo
Volta
Ilorin
Freetown
SIERRA LEONE
Bo
Nzérékoré
IVORY COAST
Bouaké
GHANA
TOGO
Porto Novo
Kumasi
Cotonou
Daloa
Yamoussoukro
Lagos
Monrovia
Accra
Lomé
LIBERIA
Abidjan
Port
Harper
San-Pédro
Sekondi-Takoradi
Gulf of Guinea

Etna
3340
Catania
Sicilia
Ionian Sea
Athens
(Athína)
Kikládes
Antalya
Bizerte
Tunis
Valletta
MALTA
5121
Iráklio
Kríti
Ródos
Nicosia
CYPRUS
Sousse
Sfax
Gafsa
I. de Jerba
Gabès
TUNISIA
MEDITERRANEAN SEA
(Ţarābulus)
Tripoli
Al Khums
Misrātah
Al Bayḑā'
Benghazi
(Banghāzī)
Surt
Ajdābiyah
Ţubruq
Al Maḩallah
al Kubrā
Port Said
(Būr Sa'īd)
Alexandria
(Al Iskandarīyah)
(Al Jīzah) Giza
Pyramids
Al Fayyūm
Cairo
(Al Qāhirah)
Suez
Al Minyā
Asyūţ
Nile
Tripolitania
Cyrenaica
Ghudāmis
Edjeléh
Sabhah
LIBYA
EGYPT
(MIŞR)
Aş Şaḩrā' al Libīyah
(Libyan Desert)
Al Kufrah
Djanet
Abu Simbel
Al Uwaynāt
Wādī Halfā
SAHARA
Tibesti
Zouar
3415
Emi Koussi
Ténéré
Aïr
Faya
Fada
Dunqulah
NIGER
ERG
CHAD
Omdurman
(Umm Durmān)
Nguigmi
Lake Chad
Zinder
Abéché
Al Fāshir
Al Ubayyid
Wad Madani
Kano
Maiduguri
N'Djamena
SUDAN
White Nile
Bauchi
Chari
Birao
Bongor
Malakāl
NIGERIA
Garoua
Abuja
Benue
Sarh
Ndélé
Wāw
Makurdi
CENTRAL AFRICAN
REPUBLIC
Ngaoundéré
Bamenda
Bouar
Bambari
Bangassou
Jūbā
CAMEROON
Mt. Cameroon
4100
Bangui
Berbérati
Ubangui
Bioko I.
Malabo
Douala
Yaoundé
EQUATORIAL
GUINEA
Lisala
Buta

Ankara
Sivas
Jerevan
Bursa
TURKEY
(TÜRKIYE)
Erzurum
5137
Nachičevan
Afyon
Elâzığ
Tabrīz
Izmir
Kayseri
Van
Aegean Sea
Gaziantep
Orūmīyeh
Antalya
Adana
Mosul
(Al Mawşil)
Kiklādes
Aleppo
(Ḩalab)
Kirkūk
Al Lādhiqīyah
Dayr az Zawr
Hamadān
Ródos
Iráklio
Nicosia
SYRIA
Tigris
(Dijlah)
Kriti
Homs (Ḩimş)
Euphrates
CYPRUS
LEBANON
3048
Baghdad
Beirut
Damascus
Haifa
IRAQ
Al Ḩillah
(Al Furāt)
ISRAEL
Al Maḩallah
al Kubrā
Port Said
(Būr Sa'īd)
Tel Aviv
Amman
Ţubruq
Jerusalem
Al Ḩadīthah
JORDAN
Alexandria
(Al Iskandarīyah)
Al Ismā'īlīyah
Basra
(Al Basrah)
(Al Jīzah) Giza
Suez
(Az Suways)
Pyramids
Al Fayyūm
Cairo
(Al Qāhirah)
Al 'Aqabah
Sinai
2637
An Nafūd
Al Minyā
Tabūk
Ḩā'il
Asyūţ
Nile
Buraydah
As Şahrā' al Lībīyah
(Libyan Desert)
EGYPT
(MIŞR)
Luxor
(Al Uqşur)
Riyadh
Medina
(Al Madīnah)
Aswān
Red Sea
Al Kufrah
Mecca
(Makkah)
SAUDI
Abu Simbel
Jeddah
(AL 'ARABĪYAH
Al Uwaynāt
Wādī Halfā
Aţ Ţā'if
Port Sudan
(Būr Sūdān)
2635
Dunqulah
3133
Abhā
Atbarah
Abā Sa'ūd
Qīzān
Fada
Omdurman
(Umm Durmān)
San'a
Khartoum
Mitsiwa
3666
Kassalā
Asmera
Al Ḩudaydah
Wad Madanī
Ta'izz
Al Fāshir
Al Ubayyid
Blue Nile
Aseb
Aden
Gonder
DJIBOUTI
Djibouti
White Nile
SUDAN
Dese
Berbera
Birao
Dire Dawa
Malakāl
Hargeysa
Addis Ababa
Wāw
Gambela
ETHIOPIA
Shashemene
Bangassou
Jūbā

TURKMEN REP.
Samarkand
TADZHIKISTAN
7495
Pik Kommunizma
Pamir
Aščhabad
Dušanbe
Amudarja
Gorgān
Damāvand
5604
Mashhad
Mazār-e Sharīf
Khānābād
K2
8611
Bāmīān
5143
Kabul
Dasht-e Kavīr
Qom
Herāt
Islamabad
Srīnagar
Ghaznī
Peshāwar
Rāwalpindi
Jammu
Bīrjand
AFGHANISTAN
Gujrānwāla
Lahore
Amritsar
Yazd
Qandahār
Faisalabad
IRAN
Ludhiāna
PUNJAB
Kermān
Quetta
Multān
Shīrāz
Zāhedān
Būshehr
Bam
4042
PAKISTAN
Bīkāner
New Delhi
Bandar-e 'Abbās
Sukkur
RĀJASTHĀN
Ajmer
Gulf
Indus
Jodhpur
BAHRAIN
Manama
Dubai
Pasni
Doha
Hyderābād
Udaipur
QATAR
Gulf of Oman
Karāchi
Abu Dhabi
Al Ain
GUJARAT
Muscat
Gāndhīnagar
Ujjain
UNITED ARAB EMIRATES
3019
Ahmadābād
Nizwā
Şūr
Rājkot
Vadodara
Porbandar
OMAN
Sūrat
Al Maşīrah
Nāshik
Khālī
Bombay
Pune
Şalālah
ARABIAN SEA
Panaji
Al Mukallā
3985
Mangalore
Aden
Socotra
(Suquţrá)
(YEMEN)
Bosaso
Amindivi Is.
(INDIA)
Laccadive Is.
(INDIA)
Laccadive
Ihavandiffulu At.
1594
1938
Malosmadulu At.

NIGER
CHAD
SUDA
NIGERIA
CENTRAL AFRICAN REPUBLIC
CAMEROON
EQUATORIAL GUINEA
SAO TOME AND PRINCIPE
GABON
CONGO
ZAIRE
ANGOLA
ZAMB
ZIMBA
Agadez
Tahoua
Zinder
Nguigmi
Lake Chad
Faya
Fada
Abéché
Al Fāshir
N'Djamena
Sokoto
Kano
Maiduguri
Kaduna
Bauchi
Abuja
Niger
Benue
Ilorin
Oshogbo
Ibadan
Lagos
Makurdi
Enugu
Benin City
Port Harcourt
Garoua
Bongor
Chari
Sarh
Birao
Ndélé
Wāw
Ngaoundéré
Bouar
Bamenda
Bambari
Bangassou
Bangui
Mt. Cameroon
4100
Bioko I.
Malabo
Douala
Yaoundé
Berbérati
Ubangui
Lisala
Buta
Bata
Ouesso
Basankusu
Kisangani
Libreville
Makokou
São Tomé
Mbandaka
Port-Gentil
Boende
Ikela
Lambaréné
Franceville
Congo
Zaire
Pagalu
Brazzaville
Kasai
Bukavu
Kindu
Loubomo
Pointe-Noire
Kinshasa
Kikwit
Cabinda
(ANG.)
Matadi
Kananga
Mbuji-Mayi
Luanda
N'dalatando
Saurimo
Kamina
Kolwezi
Likasi
Lobito
Luena
Huambo
Kitwe
Menongue
Zambezi
Namibe
Mongu
Lusaka
Livingstone
Victoria Falls
Tsumeb

Abā Sa'ūd
Qīzān
Şalāla
Khartoum
Mitsiwa
San'a
Say'ūn
3666
YEMEN
Kassalā
Asmera
Al Hudaydah
Al Mukallā
Ta'izz
Blue Nile
White Nile
Aseb
Aden
Gonder
Gulf of Aden
Socotra
(Suquţrá)
(YEMEN)
DJIBOUTI
Djibouti
Dese
Bosaso
Berbera
Dire Dawa
Gardo
Hargeysa
Addis Ababa
Gambela
ETHIOPIA
Galcaio
Shashemene
1594
SOMALIA
Belet Huen
Lodwar
Moyale
Gulu
Marsabit
Mogadishu
(Muqdisho)
UGANDA
4321
Mt. Elgon
Kitale
KENYA
Nanyuki
5199
Mt. Kenya
Kisumu
Kisimaio
Victoria
Nairobi
Mwanza
Mtito Andei
Mt.
Kilimanjaro
5895
Mombasa
Arusha
Victoria
Tabora
Tanga
Pemba I.
Zanzibar
Zanzibar I.
TANZANIA
Dodoma
SEYCHELLES
Dar es Salaam
Mafia I.
Mbeya
Aldabra I.
Lindi
Ngazidja
Songea
COMOROS
Moroni
Ndzouani
Mzuzu
Malawi
Antsiranana
Dzaoudzi
Pemba
Mayotte
(FR.)
MALAWI
Lilongwe
2876
Tsaratanana
Moçambique
Mahajanga
I. Tromelin
(FR.)
Zambezi
Blantyre
Nampula
Channel
Tete
MADAGASCAR
Juan
de Nova
(FR.)
Toamasina
Quelimane
Antananarivo
4910

Lambaréné
Franceville
Boende
Ikela
Zaire
Congo
Z A I R E
Kigali
Bukavu
Kindu
BURUNDI
Brazzaville
Loubomo
Pointe-Noire
Kinshasa
Kikwit
Kasai
Cabinda
(ANG.)
Matadi
Kananga
Mbuji-Mayi
Kalemie
Luanda
N'dalatando
Saurimo
Kamina
Kolwezi
Likasi
ANGOLA
Lubumbash
Lobito
Luena
Huambo
Kitwe
Ndola
Zambezi
Menongue
Z A M B I
Kabwe
Namibe
Mongu
Lusaka
Livingstone
Victoria Falls
Tsumeb
ZIMBABW
Maun
NAMIBIA
2579
Bulawayo
Francistown
Windhoek
Gobabis
BOTSWANA
Walvisbaai
(S.A.)
Messina
Kalahari
Desert
Pietersbu
Gaborone
Pretoria
Benoni
Johannesburg
Keetmanshoop
Lüderitz
Vereeniging
Springs
Vaal
Kroonstad
Ladysmith
Upington
Kimberley
Orange
LESOTHO
3482
Bloemfontein
Maseru
Springbok
SOUTH
AFRICA
Drakensberg
Port S
Umtata
Queenstown
Malmesbury
East London
Worcester
Oudtshoorn
Cape Town
Mossel Bay
Port Elizabeth
Cape of
Good Hope

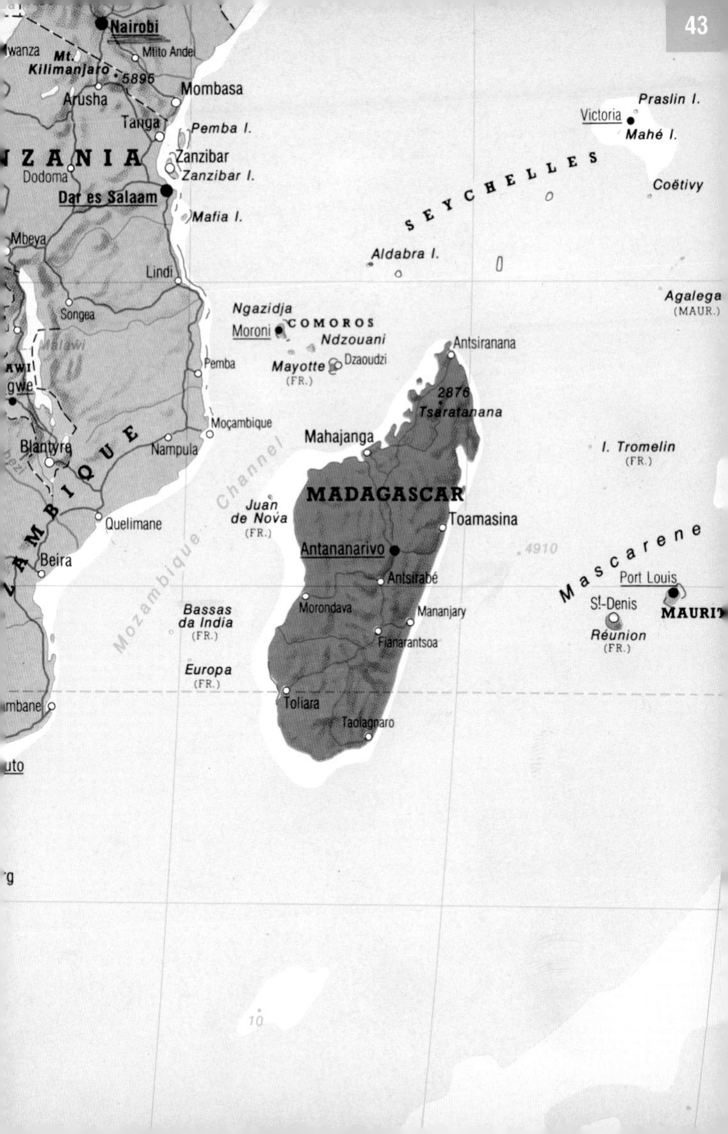

Nairobi
Mwanza
Mt. Kilimanjaro 5895
Mtito Andei
Mombasa
Arusha
Tanga
Pemba I.
TANZANIA
Zanzibar
Zanzibar I.
Dodoma
Dar es Salaam
Mafia I.
Mbeya
Lindi
Songea
Malawi
MALAWI
Lilongwe
Pemba
MOZAMBIQUE
Moçambique
Nampula
Blantyre
Quelimane
Beira
Inhambane
Maputo
Praslin I.
Victoria
Mahé I.
SEYCHELLES
Coëtivy
Aldabra I.
Agalega (MAUR.)
Ngazidja
COMOROS
Moroni
Ndzouani
Mayotte (FR.)
Dzaoudzi
Antsiranana
2876
Tsaratanana
Mahajanga
Mozambique Channel
I. Tromelin (FR.)
MADAGASCAR
Juan de Nova (FR.)
Toamasina
Antananarivo
4910
Antsirabé
Mascarene
Port Louis
MAURITIUS
St-Denis
Réunion (FR.)
Morondava
Mananjary
Fianarantsoa
Bassas da India (FR.)
Europa (FR.)
Toliara
Taolagnaro
10

6290
Prince Edward I.
(S.A.)
Marion I.
(S.A.)
I.
I.
2607
C.
Molod'ožnaja
(U.S.S.R.)
2300
Enderby
Syowa
(JAP.)
Prince Olav Coast
Maud Land

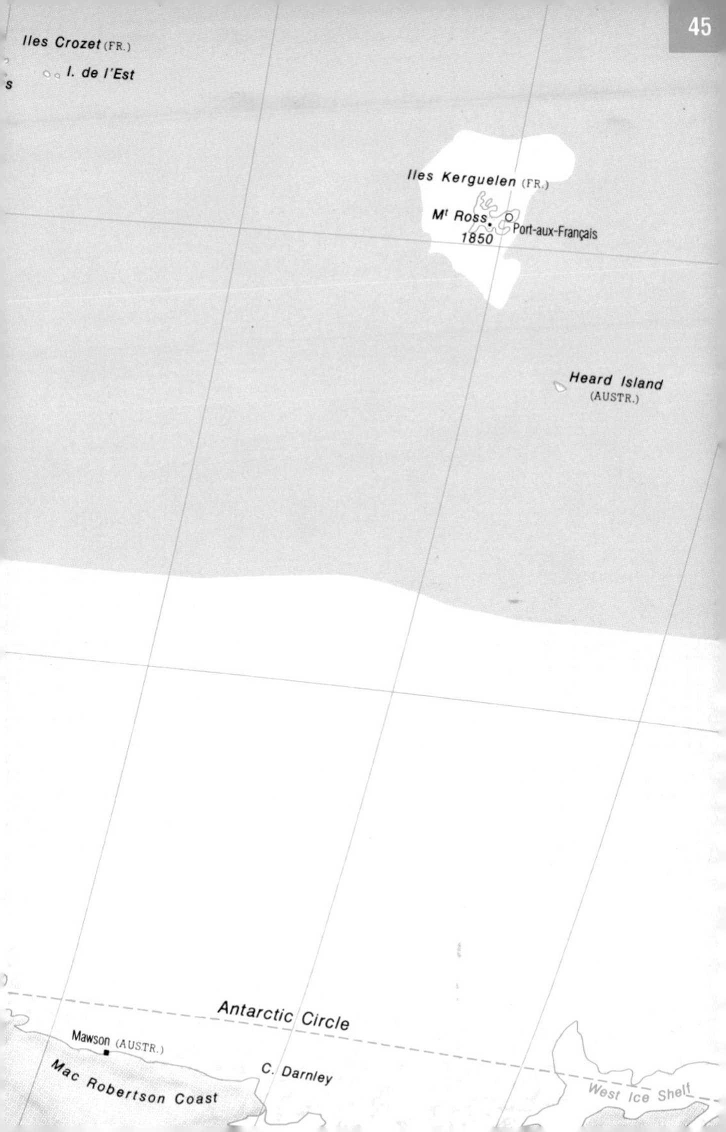

Iles Crozet (FR.)

I. de l'Est

s

Iles Kerguelen (FR.)

Mt Ross 1850

Port-aux-Français

Heard Island (AUSTR.)

Antarctic Circle

Mawson (AUSTR.)

C. Darnley

Mac Robertson Coast

West Ice Shelf

O. Komsomolec
O. Okt'abr'skoj Revol'ucii
O. Šmidta
O. Ušakova
O. Pioner
O. Bol'ševik
O. Mal. Ta
Mys Čel'us
North Land
(Severnaja Zeml'a)
Pr. Vil'kickogo
O. Vize
Arch. Nordenšel'da
O-va Sergeja Kirova
SEA
More)
Mys Želanija
Poluostrov
O-va Arktičeskogo Instituta
Ust'-Tareja
Severo - Sibi
O. Vil'kickogo
Dikson
O. Belyj
O. Sibir'akova
Jenisejskij Zaliv
RA
arskoje
Obskaja Guba
Dudinka
Noril'sk
Jenisej
Igarka
gač
Bajdarackaja G.
mderma
Novyj Port
Tazovskij
Chal'mer-Ju
Vorkuta
Labytnangi
Salechard
Turuchansk
(ROSSIJA)
Nadym
Tarko-Sale
1883
Ber'ozovo
OF
SO

New Sibe
(Novosibi
O. Bel'kovskij
O. Kotel'nyj
O. Stolbovoj
L'achov
LAPTEV SEA
(More Laptevych)
O-va Petra
O. Bol. Begičev
Olen'okskij Zaliv
G. Buor-Chaja
Nordvik
Chatangskij Zaliv
Tiksi
Nizmennost'
Chatanga
Olen'ok
Šikťach
Lena
Kotuj
Olen'ok
Žigansk
CENTRAL SIBERIAN PLATEAU
Arctic Circle
(Srednesibirskoje Ploskogorje)
Vil'uj
N'urba
Tura
Niž. Tunguska
Mirnyj
Suntar
SOCIALIST
SOCIALISTIČESKICH
Lensk

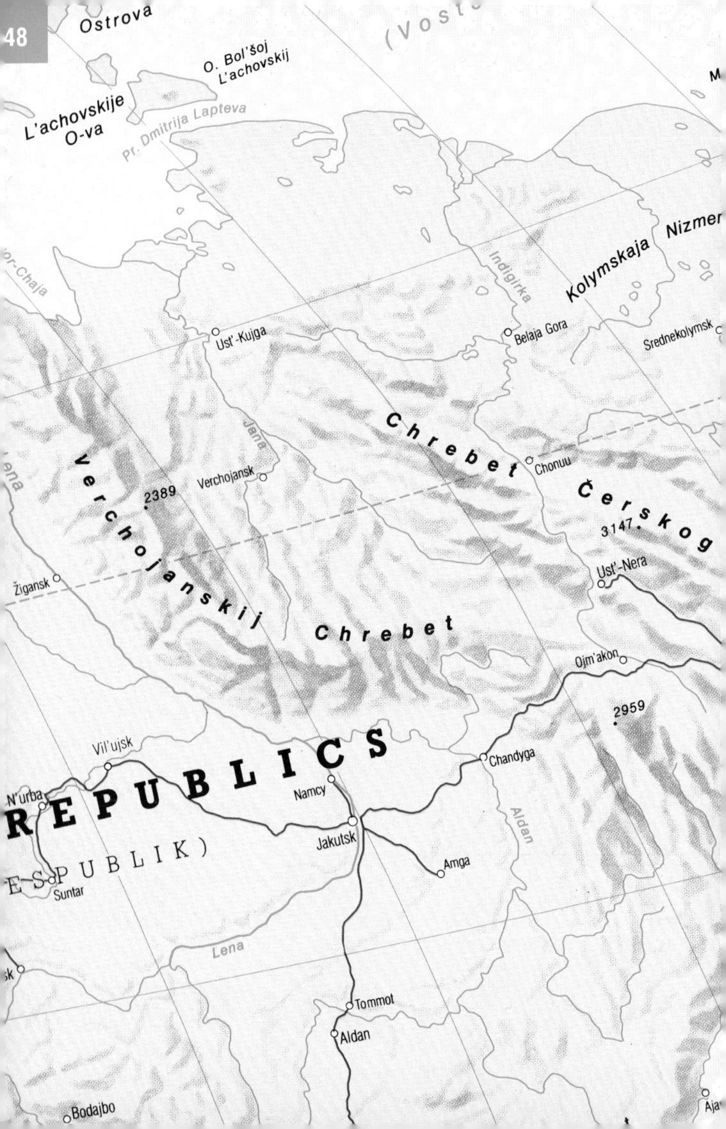
Ostrova
O. Bol'šoj L'achovskij
L'achovskije O-va
Pr. Dmitrija Lapteva
Indigirka
Kolymskaja Nizmer
Ust'-Kujga
Belaja Gora
Srednekolymsk
Jana
Chrebet
Chonuu
Verchojansk
Verchojanskij
2389
Čerskog
3147
Ust'-Nera
Žigansk
Chrebet
Ojm'akon
2959
Vil'ujsk
REPUBLICS
Chandyga
N'urba
Namcy
Jakutsk
Aldan
PUBLIK)
Amga
Suntar
Lena
Tommot
Aldan
Bodajbo

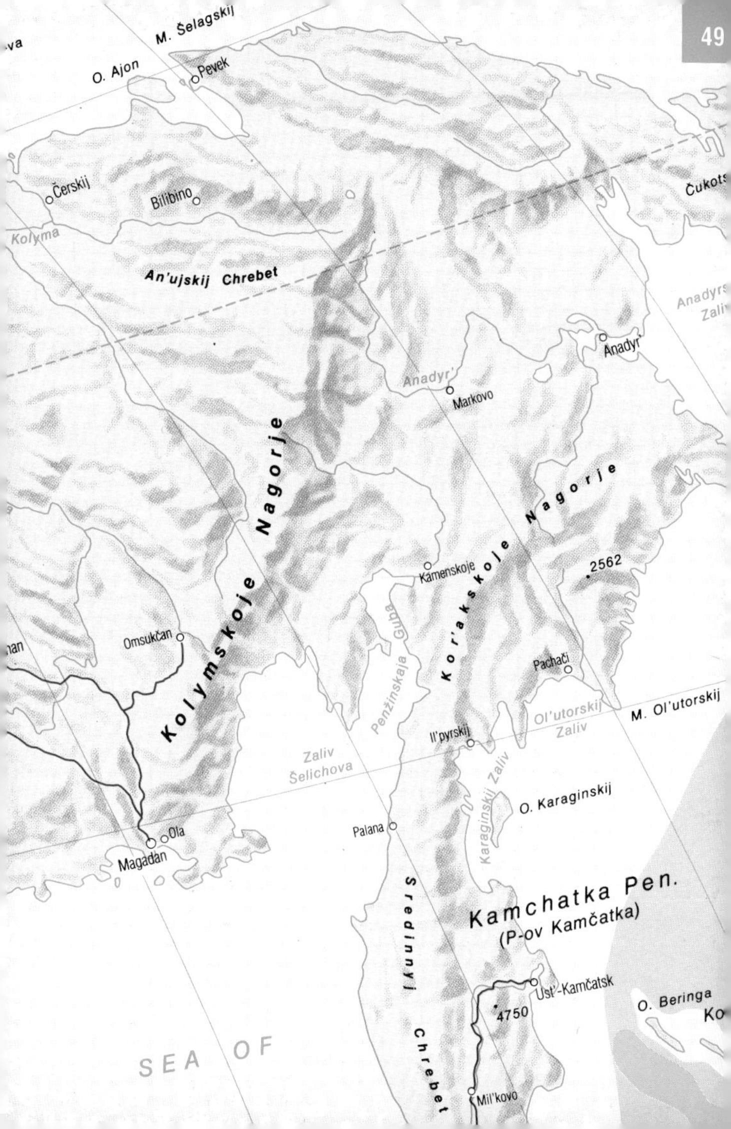
M. Šelagskij
O. Ajon
Pevek
Čerskij
Bilibino
Kolyma
An'ujskij Chrebet
Čukots
Anadyrs Zaliv
Anadyr'
Anadyr'
Markovo
Kolymskoje Nagorje
Kor'akskoje Nagorje
2562
Kamenskoje
Omsukčan
Penžinskaja Guba
Pachači
Ol'utorskij Zaliv
M. Ol'utorskij
Il'pyrskij
Zaliv Šelichova
Karaginskij Zaliv
O. Karaginskij
Palana
Ola
Magadan
Sredinnyj Chrebet
Kamchatka Pen.
(P-ov Kamčatka)
Ust'-Kamčatsk
4750
O. Beringa
SEA OF
Mil'kovo

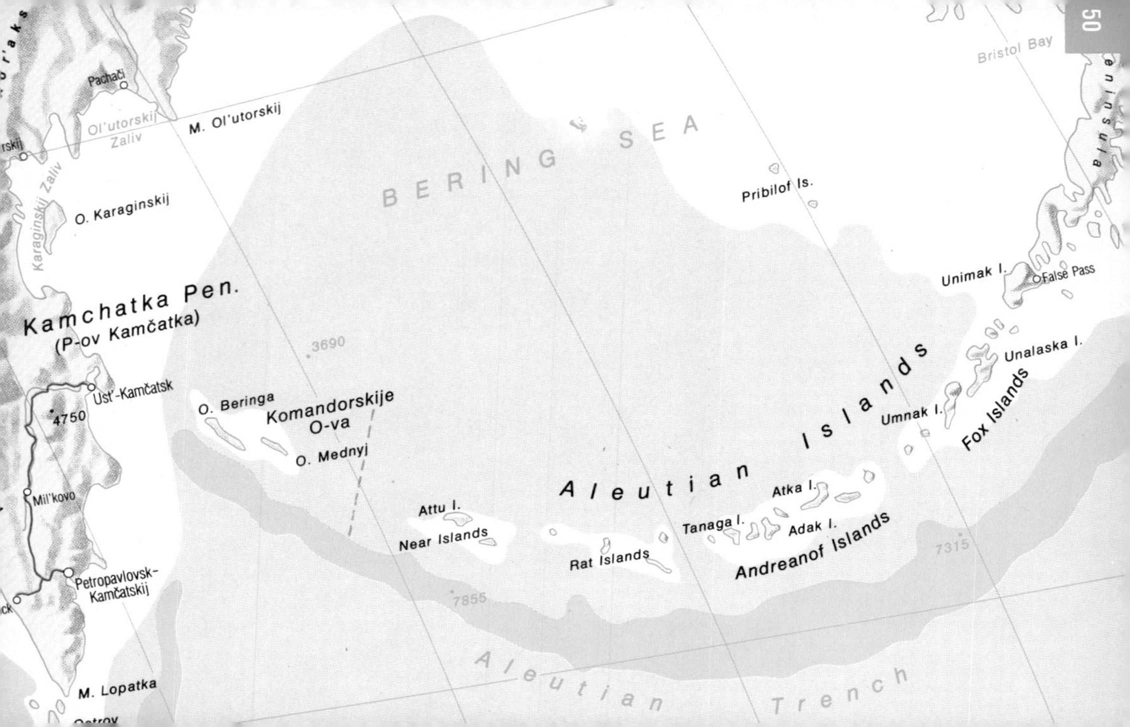
Pachači
Ol'utorskij Zaliv
M. Ol'utorskij
BERING SEA
Bristol Bay
Karaginskij Zaliv
O. Karaginskij
Pribilof Is.
Kamchatka Pen.
(P-ov Kamčatka)
Unimak I.
False Pass
3690
Unalaska I.
Ust'-Kamčatsk
4750
O. Beringa
Komandorskije O-va
O. Mednyj
Aleutian Islands
Umnak I.
Fox Islands
Mil'kovo
Attu I.
Near Islands
Rat Islands
Tanaga I.
Atka I.
Adak I.
Andreanof Islands
7315
Petropavlovsk-Kamčatskij
7855
M. Lopatka
Aleutian Trench

O. Simušir
Urup
9783
Kuril Trench
NORTH PACIFIC
5

SOVETSKICH
Bajkit
Komsa
Podkamennaja Tunguska
urgut
Nižnevartovsk
Ob'
Jenisej
PLAIN
Angara
ERIAN
Jenisejsk
Ust'-Ili
Ravnina)
Kargasok
Kolpaševo
irskaja
Tasejevo
Tegul'det
Kansk
Ačinsk
Tajšet
Tara
Tomsk
Krasnojarsk
Kemerovo
Kujbyšev
Novosibirsk
Prokopjevsk
Novokuzneck
Abakan
Omsk
Ob'
Barnaul
Bijsk
Kyzyl
Jenisej
Pavlodar
Celinograd
Irtyš
Ust'-Kamenogorsk
4506
Semipalatinsk
Altai Mts.
Temirtau
Karaganda
AN
Altay
Zajsan
4231
ezkazgan
Balchaš
Ozero Balchaš
Karamay
Shihezi
Urumchi (Ürümqi)
Yining
5445
Shan
Alma-Ata
Tian
Hami
Džambul
Frunze
Turpan
Prževal'sk
Pik Pobedy
7439
Čimkent
KIRGHIZIA
Korla
Kuqa
Lop Nur
Taškent
Namangan
Tarim
Andižan
Aksu
SINKIANG
Kokand
Taklimakan Shamo
Kashi
TADZHIKISTAN
7495
Pik Kommunizma
Qiemo
Dušanbe
Pamir
Hotan
Shan

Tommot
Aldan
Bodajbo
Kirensk
2800
Stanovoj
Ust'-Kut
Lena
Tynda
Ozero Bajkal
Bagdarin
Kurumkan
Skovorodino
Mogoča
Amur
Heilong Jiang
Balagansk
Tahe
Sretensk
Čita
Angarsk
Irkutsk
Ulan-Ude
Da Hinggan Ling
K'achta
Borz'a
Kyra
2523
Manzhouli
Hailar
Darhan
Zalantun
Choybalsan
Ulan Bator
MONGOLIA
Baichen
Saynshand
Xilinhot
Erenhot
Dalandzadgad
Gobi Desert
INNER MONGOLIA
Shenya
LIAO
Hohhot
Zhangjiakou
Jinzhou
Linhe
Chengde
Qinhuangdao
Yumen
Baotou
Peking
(Beijing)
Datong
Tangshan
Tientsin
(Tianjin)
Shizuishan
Baoding
HOPEH
Taiyuan
Shijiazhuang
Yinchuan
Yulin
KANSU
NINGSIA HUI
Wuwei
Xingtai
Zibo
Weifang
Xining
SHANSI
Jinan
Golmud
Qiqi
Char

SEA
OKHOTSK
Stanovoj Chrebet
2520
Ajan
Tynda
Skovorodino
Amur
Jiang
Tahe
Ekimčan
Svobodnyj
Blagoveščensk
Oblučje
Šantarskije O-va
M. Jelizavety
Nikolajevsk-na-Amure
Ocha
Komsomol'sk-na-Amure
Amur
Chabarovsk
Sovetskaja Gavan'
Tatarskij Proliv
Aleksandrovsk-Sachalinskij
Ostrov Sachalin
Poronajsk
Južno-Sachalinsk
M. Aniva
La Pérouse Strait
Mil'kovo
Petropavlovsk-Kamčatskij
Ust'-Bol'šereck
rebet
M. Lopatka
Ostrov Paramušir
Kuril Islands
(Kurilskije O-va)
1394
O. Simušir
O. Urup
O. Iturup
O. Kunašir
O. Šikotan
9783
Kuril Trench
Wakkanai
Asahikawa
2290
Sapporo
Kusiro
Nemuro
Hokkaidō
Hakodate
Da Hinggan Ling
Hailar
Nenjiang
Zalantun
Bei'an
Hegang
HEILUNGKIANG
Jiamusi
Qiqihar
Anda
Manchuria
Harbin
Jixi
Baicheng
Mudanjiang
KIRIN
Jilin
Changchun
Siping
Liaoyuan
Yanji
Dal'nerečensk
Dal'negorsk
Rudnaja Pristan'
Ussurijsk
Vladivostok
Nachodka
LIA

NORTH KOREA
(CHOSŎN)
Pyongyang
Hŭngnam
Kaesŏng
Seoul
Samch'ŏk
Inch'ŏn
SOUTH KOREA
(HAN KUK)
Taejŏn
Taegu
Kwangju
Pusan
Cheju-do
Yellow Sea
East China Sea
Sea of Japan
3063
Honsyū
Akita
Morioka
Sendai
Niigata
Utunomiya
Kanazawa
Tōkyō
Fujiyama 3776
Yokohama
Kyōto
Nagoya
Hiroshima
Kōbe
Ōsaka
Kita-kyūsyū
Hukuoka
Matuyama
Sikoku
Nagasaki
Kumamoto
Kyūsyū
Kagosima
Ōsumi Sō.
Hatizyō Za
JAPAN
(NIPPON)
Japan Trench
Izu Syotō
Izu Trench
9850
Nanpō Syotō
(JAP.)
Bonin Trench
Bonin Is.
(Ogasawara Guntō)
Kazan Rettō
Amami Ō Sa
Okinawa
Naha
Ryukyu Islands (JAP.)
(Nansei Syotō)
Sakisima Syotō
Daitō Zima
(JAP.)
Taipei
TAIWAN
(FORMOSA)
Kaohsiung
Taiwan Str.
Jinzhou
Chengde
Qinhuangdao
Dandong
Tangshan
Tientsin
(Tianjin)
Dalian
Shijiazhuang
Yantai
Zibo
Weifang
Jinan
Qingdao
SHANTUNG
(Huang He)
Jining
Zaozhuang
Lianyungang
Zhengzhou
Xuzhou
KIANGSU
Huainan
Nanking (Nanjing)
Suzhou
Shanghai
Hefei
Wuhu
Wuhan
ANHWEI
Hangzhou
Ningbo
Jiujiang
CHEKIANG
Jingdezhen
Nanchang
Wenzhou
KIANGSI
Nanping
Hengyang
Fuzhou
Ganzhou
FUKIEN
Quanzhou
Xiamen
KWANGTUNG
(Guangzhou)
Canton
Shantou
Hong Kong
(U.K.)
Macau

Kashi
Qiemo
TSINGHAI
Pamir
Hotan
Golmud
Kunlun Shan
K2
8611
7723
C
(ZH
JAMMU AND KASHMIR
Islamabad
Srīnagar
Leh
Ladakh
Rāwalpindi
Jammu
Plateau of Tibet
Gujrānwāla
HIMACHAL PRAD.
Shiquanhe
Lahore
Amritsar
Simla
Himalayas
TIBET (XIZANG)
Faisalabad
Ludhiāna
Chandīgarh
PUNJAB
7816
Multān
Sahāranpur
Xigazê
Lhasa
HARYĀNA
8180
Delhi
Meerut
Bīkāner
NEPAL
8848 Mt. Everest
New Delhi
Bareilly
Kathmandu
Thimbu
BHUTAN
ARUNACHAL P.
Sadiy
Itānagar
RĀJASTHĀN
UTTAR PRAD.
SIKKIM
Patan
Āgra
Taj Mahal
Lucknow
Darjeeling
Brahmaputra
Ajmer
Jaipur
Gorakhpur
ASSAM
Jodhpur
Kānpur
Guwāhāti
Gwalior
Ganges
Patna
Ganga
Shillong
Udaipur
Allahābād
Benares (Vārānasi)
BIHĀR
Gaya
BANGLADESH
Dhaka
Imphāl
GUJARAT
MADHYA PRAD.
Āsānsol
WEST BENGAL
Agartala
Gāndhīnagar
Ujjain
Bhopāl
Jabalpur
Jamshedpur
Ahmadābād
Khulna
Rājkot
Indore
INDIA (BHĀRAT)
Calcutta
Chittagong
Vadodara
Kharagpur
Sūrat
Raipur
Nāshik
Ajanta
Nāgpur
Bhubaneshwar
Paga
Sittwe
Aurangābād
ORISSA
Puri
Bombay
MAHĀRĀSHTRA
Pune
Solāpur
Hyderābād
Vishākhapatnam
ANDHRA PRADESH
Vijayawāda
Guntūr
Bass
BAY OF BENGAL
Panaji
Hubli
Nellore
KARNĀTAKA
Bangalore
Madras
Mangalore
Mysore
Pondicherry
Port
TAMIL NADU
Amindivi Is. (INDIA)
Coimbatore
Tiruchchirāppalli
Laccadive Is. (INDIA)
KERALA
Cochin
Madurai
Jaffna
Laccadive Sea
Trincomalee
Trivandrum
C. Comorin
SRI LANKA (CEYLON)
Kandy
Nicobar Is. (INDIA)
Ihavandiffulu At.
Colombo
2529
Miladummadulu Atoll
Galle
Malosmadulu At.

Taiyuan
Shijiazhuang
Yinchuan
Yulin
NINGSIA HUI
Wuwei
Xingtai
Zibo
Weifang
Jinan
Qingdao
SHANSI
SHANTUNG
Yellow Sea
Xining
Lanzhou
Yan'an
Anyang
Jining
Zaozhuang
Lianyungang
SHENSI
Yellow R.
Linxia
Baoji
Luoyang
Zhengzhou
Xuzhou
Tianshui
Xi'an
HONAN
KIANGSU
Huang He
Nanyang
Huainan
Nanking (Nanjing)
Ankang
Xinyang
Hefei
Suzhou
Shanghai
SZECHWAN
HUPEH
Wuhu
Yangtze (Chang)
Guan Xian
Chengdu
Wanxian
Yichang
Wuhan
ANHWEI
Hangzhou
Hechuan
Shashi
Ningbo
Jiujiang
CHEKIANG
7590
Leshan
Neijiang
Jingdezhen
Chongqing
Changsha
Nanchang
Wenzhou
Jinsha
HUNAN
Xichang
Zunyi
Xiangtan
KIANGSI
KWEICHOW
Nanping
Shaoyang
Hengyang
Ganzhou
FUKIEN
Fuzhou
Lupanshui
Guiyang
Quanzhou
Taipei
Dali
Guilin
Shaoguan
Xiamen
Kunming
Taiwan Str.
Liuzhou
KWANGTUNG
YUNNAN
Wuzhou
(Guangzhou)
TAIWAN (FORMOSA)
Canton
Shantou
Gejiu
KWANGSI CHUANG
Jiang
Nanning
Hong Kong (U.K.)
Kaohsiung
Lao Cai
Macau (PORT.)
Luzon Strait
Hanoi
Beihai
Gulf of Tonkin
Zhanjiang
Haiphong
Louangphrabang
Thanh Hoa
Haikou
Chiang Mai
LAOS
Hainan Dao
Laoag
Vientiane
VIETNAM
Phitsanulok
Udon Thani
Savannakhet
Paracel Is.
Baguio
Hue
Da Nang
THAILAND (PRATHET THAI)
Mekong
Pakxe
2598
Korat
Saraburi
Manila
Tavoy
Bangkok
Angkor
Qui Nhon
Batangas
Chon Buri
Batdâmbâng
4424
Mindoro I.
Mergui
KAMPUCHEA (CAMBODIA)
Nha Trang
Gulf of Thailand
South China Sea
Phnom Penh
Palawan I.
Ho Chi Minh City
Kâmpóng Saôm
Can Tho
Pto. Princesa
Surat Thani
Con Son
Sulu Sea
Mui Bai Bung
Spratly I.
Balabac Strait
Phuket
Zamboanga
Songkhla
Kota Kinabalu
4101
George Town
Kota Bharu
MALAYSIA

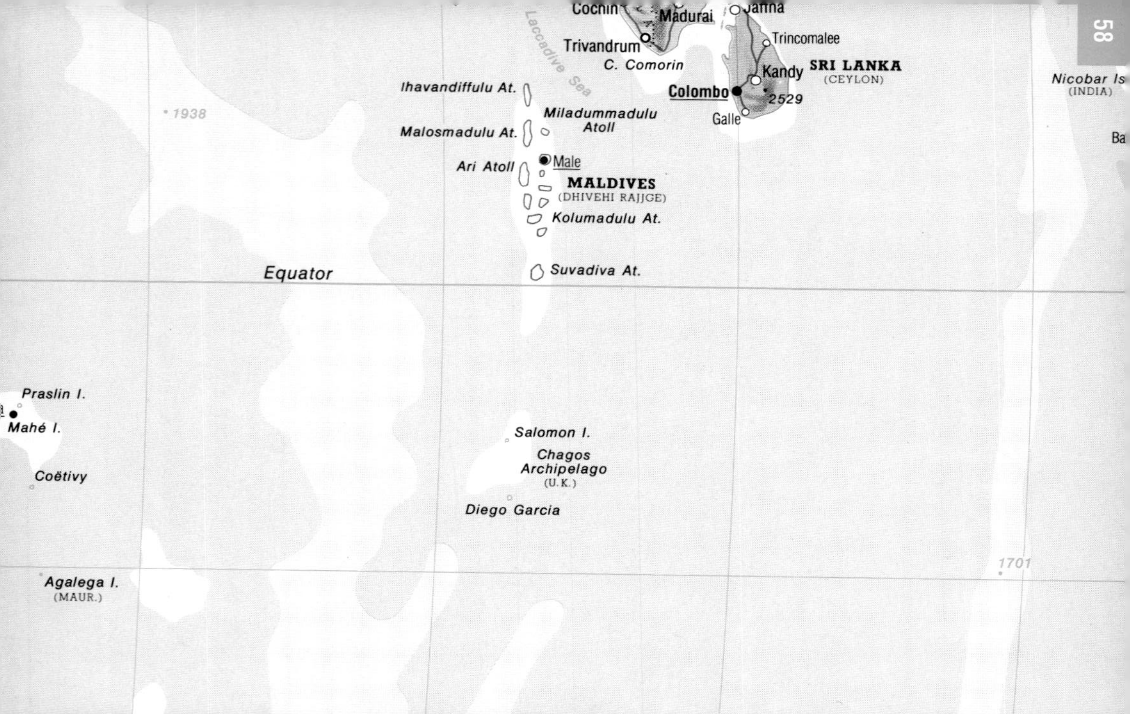
Cochin
Madurai
Jaffna
Trivandrum
Trincomalee
C. Comorin
Kandy
SRI LANKA
(CEYLON)
Nicobar Is
(INDIA)
Laccadive Sea
Ihavandiffulu At.
Colombo
2529
Galle
1938
Miladummadulu
Atoll
Malosmadulu At.
Ba
Ari Atoll
Male
MALDIVES
(DHIVEHI RAJJGE)
Kolumadulu At.
Equator
Suvadiva At.
Praslin I.
Mahé I.
Salomon I.
Chagos
Archipelago
(U.K.)
Coëtivy
Diego Garcia
1701
Agalega I.
(MAUR.)

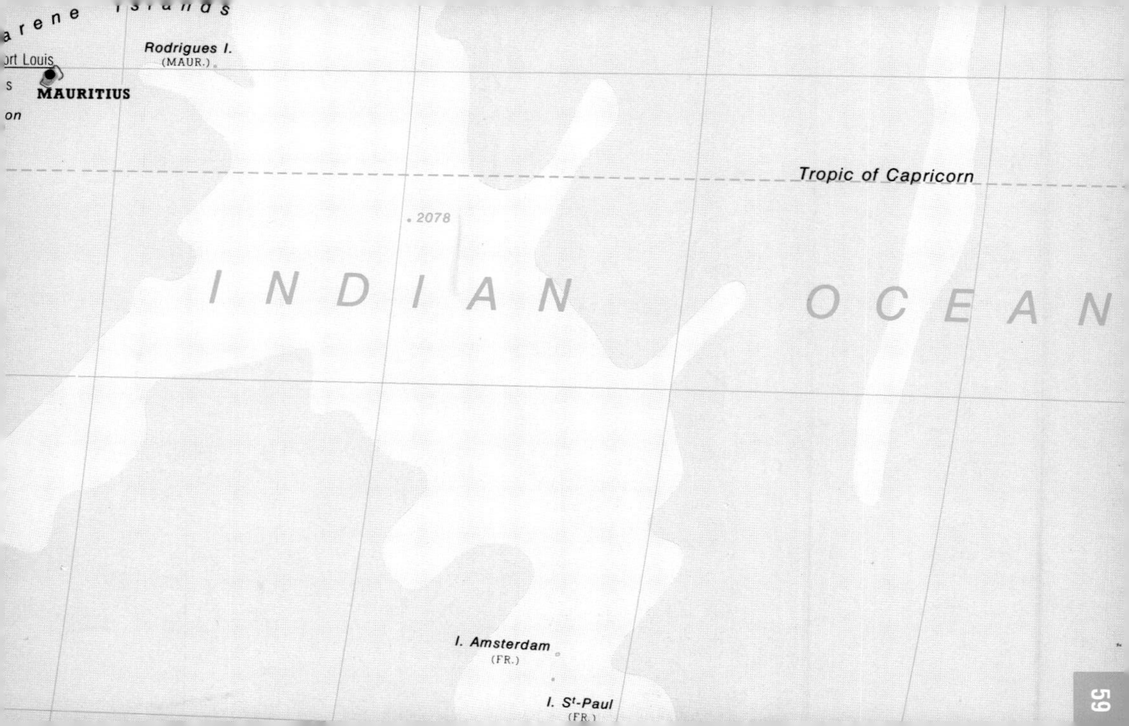
arene
Rodrigues I.
(MAUR.)
ort Louis
MAURITIUS
Tropic of Capricorn
INDIAN OCEAN
2078
I. Amsterdam
(FR.)
I. St-Paul
(FR.)

Mandalay
Pagan
Meiktila
Sittwe
Prome
Yangon
(Rangoon)
Pegu
Bassein
Moulmein
Hanoi
Beihai
Gulf of
Tonkin
Zhanjiang
Macau
(PORT.)
Haiphong
Haikou
Hainan Dao
Louangphrabang
Thanh Hoa
Chiang Mai
LAOS
Vientiane
Udon
Thani
Phitsanulok
Savannakhet
Hue
Da Nang
Paracel
THAILAND
(PRATHET THAI)
VIETNAM
Mekong
Korat
Pakxe
2598
Saraburi
Tavoy
Bangkok
Angkor
Batdâmbâng
Qui Nhon
Chon Buri
KAMPUCHEA
(CAMBODIA)
Nha Trang
Andaman Is.
(INDIA)
Port Blair
Mergui
Gulf of
Thailand
Phnom Penh
Andaman
Sea
Kâmpóng Saôm
Ho Chi Minh
City
Can Tho
South China
Surat Thani
Con Son
Mui Bai Bung
Spratly I.
Nicobar Is.
(INDIA)
Phuket
Songkhla
Kota Bharu
George Town
Banda Aceh
Ipoh
MALAYSIA
BRUNEI
Bandar Seri Begawan
Str. of Malacca
P. Natuna
Medan
2190
Kuantan
Simeulue
Kuala Lumpur
Pematangsiantar
Johor Bahru
Sibu
Paloh
Kuching
Nias
Pekanbaru
SINGAPORE
Pontianak
Borneo
(Kalimantan)
Sintang
Kep.
Lingga
Padang
Siberut
Jambi
Sumatra
(Sumatera)
3800
Bangka
Kendawangan
Palembang
Belitung
Bengkulu
IN
Telukbetung
Java Sea
Jakarta
Enggano
Selat Sunda
Semarang
Madura
Bandung
Borobudur
Surabaya
Java
(Jawa)
Yogyakarta
Malang
1701
Java Trench
Christmas I.
(AUSTR.)
7125
Cocos Is.
(AUSTR.)

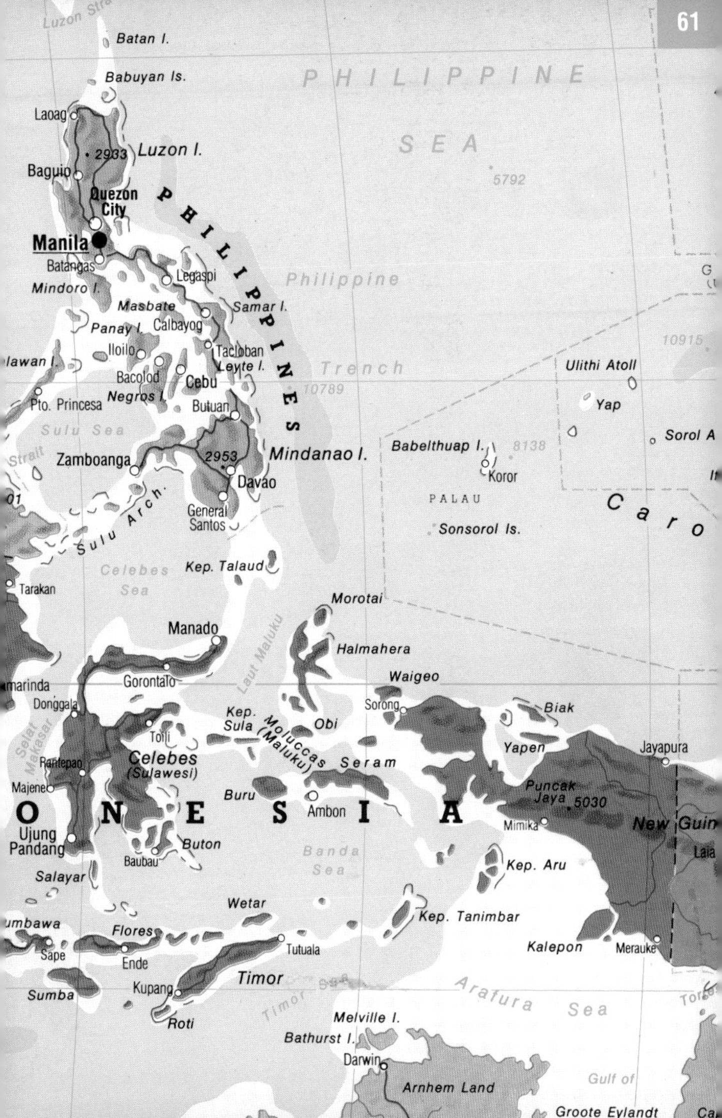

PHILIPPINE SEA
PHILIPPINES
Philippine Trench
Luzon I.
Manila
Quezon City
Mindanao I.
Davao
Zamboanga
Sulu Sea
Celebes Sea
Celebes (Sulawesi)
Moluccas (Maluku)
Halmahera
Seram
Ambon
Banda Sea
Timor
Arafura Sea
New Guin
Jayapura
Puncak Jaya 5030
PALAU
Koror
Babelthuap I.
Yap
Ulithi Atoll
Darwin
Arnhem Land
Groote Eylandt

Maug Is.
NORTHERN MARIANA ISLANDS
Agrihan
Pagan
Mariana Islands
Saipan
Tinian
Rota
GUAM (U.S.A.)
Agaña
Mariana Trench
10915
Wake (U.S.A.)
MARSHALL ISLANDS
Taongi At.
Marshall Islands
TRUST TERRITORY OF THE PACIFIC ISLANDS (U.S.A.)
Eniwetok Atoll
Bikini Atoll
Utirik At
Rongelap At.
Kwajalein At.
Wotje At
Maloelap Atoll
Majuro At.
Uliga
Arno At.
Ailinglapalap At.
Jaluit At.
Mili At.
MICRONESIA
Ulithi Atoll
Yap
Sorol At.
Lamotrek At.
Mamonuito Atoll
Hall Is.
Ifalik At.
Pulap At.
Truk Is.
Senyavin Is.
Pohnpei
Kolonia
FEDERATED STATES OF MICRONESIA
Nomoi Is.
Pingelap
Kusaie
Caroline Islands
Nukuoro At.
Kapingamarangi At.
Equator
Biak
Admiralty Is.
Manus
Yaren
NAURU
Abaiang At.
Bairiki
Gilbert Is.
KIRI

PAPUA NEW GUINEA
New Britain
Madang
Laiagam
4694
Lae
Aru
Merauke
G. of Papua
Port Moresby
Torres Strait
Sea
C. York
d'Entrecasteaux Is.
Solomon Sea
Louisiade Arch.
Tagula
Solomon Islands
Bougainville I.
Choiseul I.
Santa Isabel
SOLOMON ISLANDS
Malaita
Honiara
Guadalcanal
San Cristobal
Santa Cruz Is.
Rennell I.
Gulf of Carpentaria
Groote Eylandt
Wellesley Is.
Cape York Peninsula
Cooktown
Cairns
Great Barrier Reef
Coral Sea
5084
Banks Is.
Espiritu Santo
VANUATU
Malakula
Ambrym
Épi
Éfaté
Vila
I. Huon
Erromango
Tanna
Iles Chesterfield (FR.)
I. de Sable
Townsville
Cumberland Is.
Mount Isa
Mackay
Winton
Great Dividing Range
Barcaldine
Rockhampton
QUEENSLAND
Fraser I.
Charleville
Maryborough
Chinchilla
Iles Loyauté
Ouvéa
Lifou
Maré
Nouvelle-Calédonie (FR.)
Nouméa
7633
I. des Pins
Tropi
SOUTH PACI

Timor
Sumba
Kupang
Roti
Timor Sea
Melville I.
Bathurst I.
Darwin
Wyndham
Broome
Port Hedland
Great Sandy Desert
Tanami Desert
Tennant
Onslow
North West Cape
Hamersley Ra.
1226
Macdonn
1510
WESTERN
Carnarvon
Gibson Desert
AUSTRA
Dirk Hartogs I.
Ayers Rock 867
AUSTRALIA
Musgrave Ras.
Geraldton
Great Victoria Desert
Coolgardie
SOUTH AU
Perth
Northam
Nullarbor Plain
Kingoonya
Great Australian Bight
C. Leeuwin
Augusta
Albany
Arch. of the Recherche
Port Lincoln
Kangaroo
5200

Sea
Torres Strait
C. York
Port Moresby
d'Entrecasteaux Is.
Sea
Guadalca
Louisiade Arch.
Tagula
Rennell I.
Gulf of
Carpentaria
Groote Eylandt
Cape York Peninsula
Wellesley Is.
Great Barrier Reef
Cooktown
Cairns
Coral Sea
Great Dividing Range
Townsville
Iles Chesterfield (FR.)
Cumberland Is.
Mount Isa
Mackay
Winton
Barcaldine
Rockhampton
A
QUEENSLAND
Fraser I.
Maryborough
Charleville
Chinchilla
SO
Brisbane
Ipswich
Southport
Darling
Bourke
Armidale
Augusta
Broken Hill
Port Macquarie
Lord Howe I. (AUSTR.)
Dubbo
NEW SOUTH WALES
Range
Pirie
Orange
Newcastle
Mildura
Sydney
delaide
Hay
Goulburn
Tailem Bend
Murray
Wollongong
Great Dividing
Albury
Canberra
Bendigo
2230
Mt. Kosciusko
Mount Gambier
VICTORIA
Ballarat
Melbourne
C. Howe
Geelong
Moe
TASMAN
Bass Strait

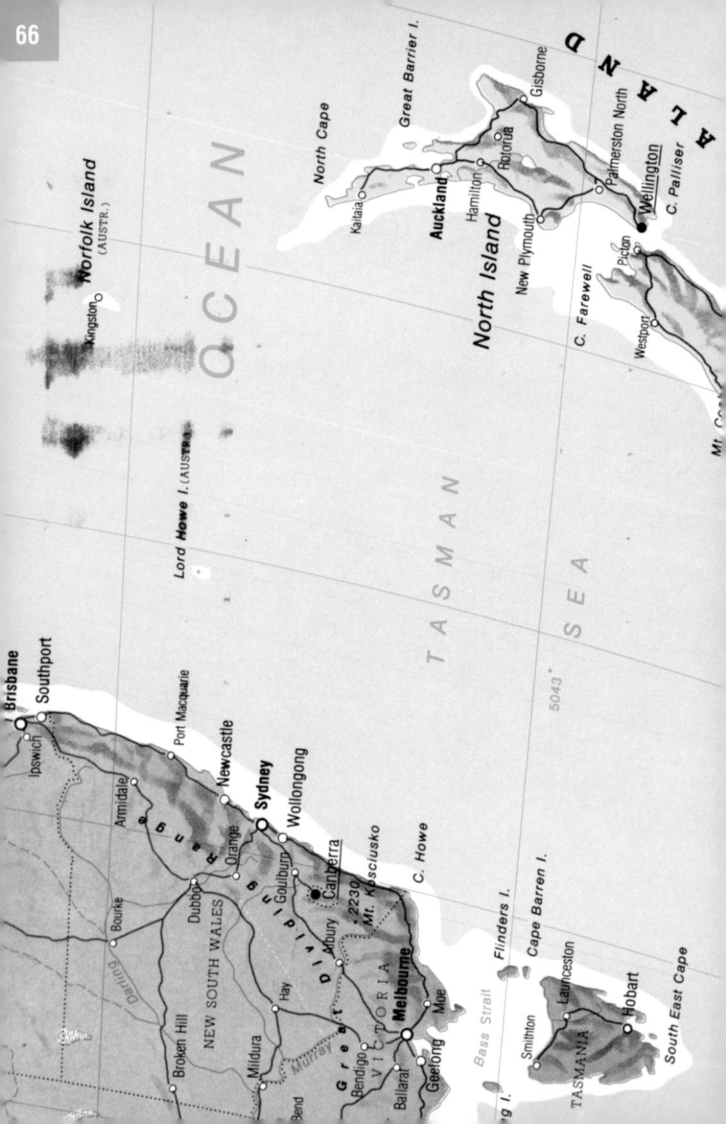

Norfolk Island
(AUSTR.)
Kingston
Lord Howe I. (AUSTR.)
North Cape
Great Barrier I.
OCEAN
TASMAN SEA
5043
Gisborne
Kaitaia
Auckland
Hamilton
Rotorua
Palmerston North
New Plymouth
North Island
Wellington
C. Palliser
Picton
C. Farewell
Westport
Mt. Cook
ZEALAND
Brisbane
Southport
Ipswich
Port Macquarie
Newcastle
Armidale
Sydney
Wollongong
Orange
Bourke
Dubbo
NEW SOUTH WALES
Goulburn
Canberra
Mt. Kosciusko
2230
C. Howe
Great Dividing Range
Darling
Broken Hill
Mildura
Murray
Hay
Albury
VICTORIA
Melbourne
Moe
Bendigo
Ballarat
Geelong
Bend
Flinders I.
Cape Barren I.
Bass Strait
Smithton
Launceston
TASMANIA
Hobart
South East Cape

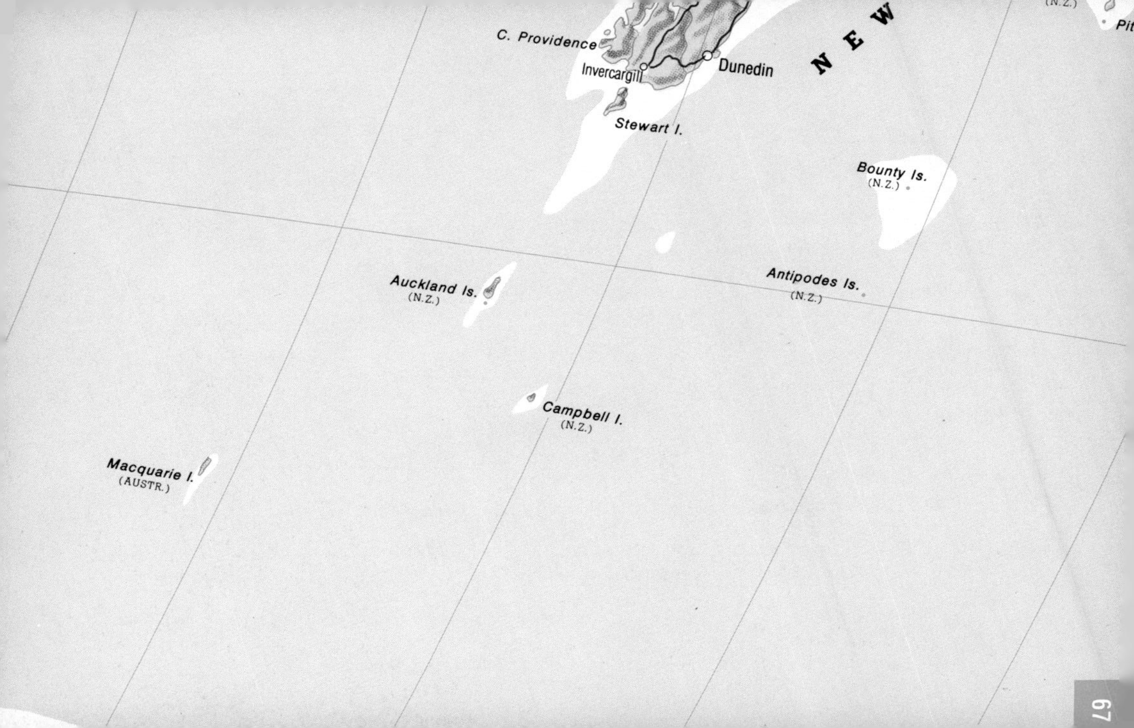

(N.Z.)

C. Providence

Invercargill

Dunedin

NEW

Stewart I.

Bounty Is.
(N.Z.)

Auckland Is.
(N.Z.)

Antipodes Is.
(N.Z.)

Campbell I.
(N.Z.)

Macquarie I.
(AUSTR.)

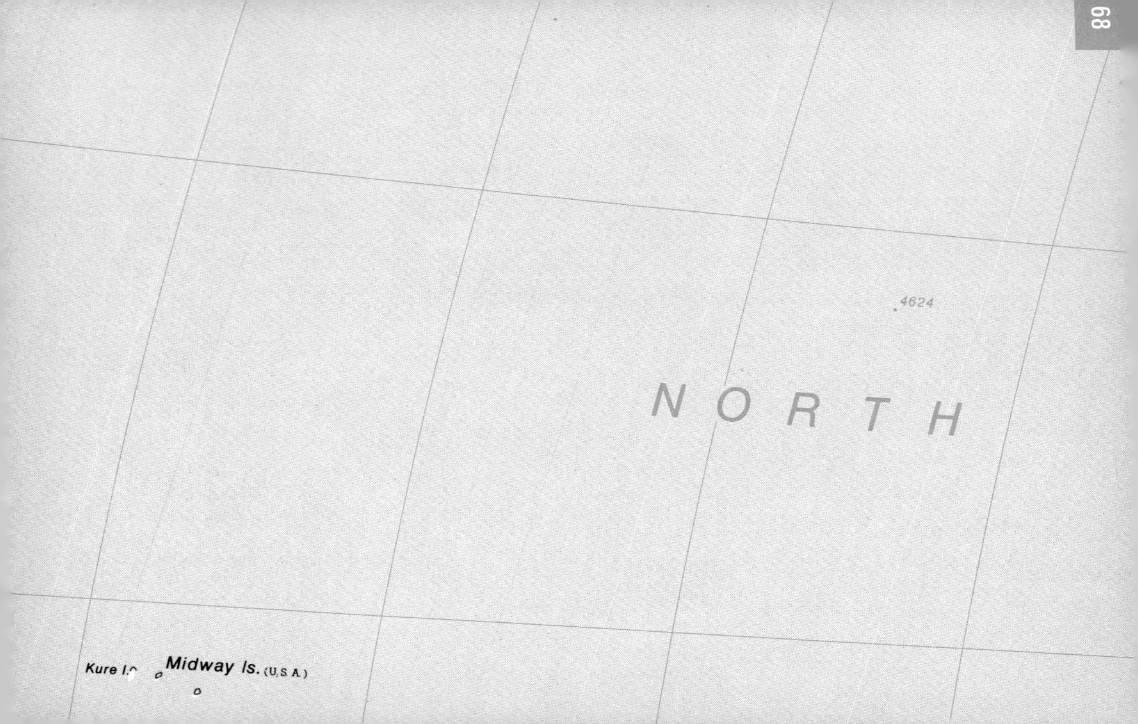

NORTH

.4624

Kure I.

Midway Is. (U.S.A.)

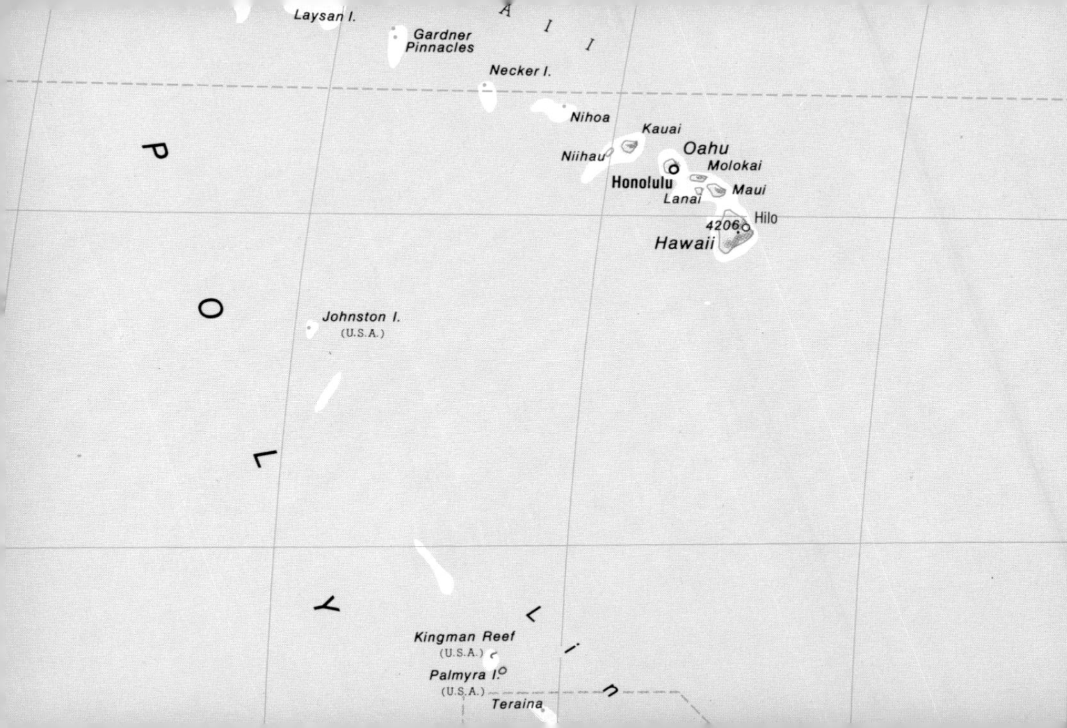

Laysan I.
Gardner Pinnacles
Necker I.
Nihoa
Niihau
Kauai
Oahu
Honolulu
Molokai
Lanai
Maui
Hilo
4206
Hawaii
Johnston I. (U.S.A.)
Kingman Reef (U.S.A.)
Palmyra I. (U.S.A.)
Teraina
P O L Y N

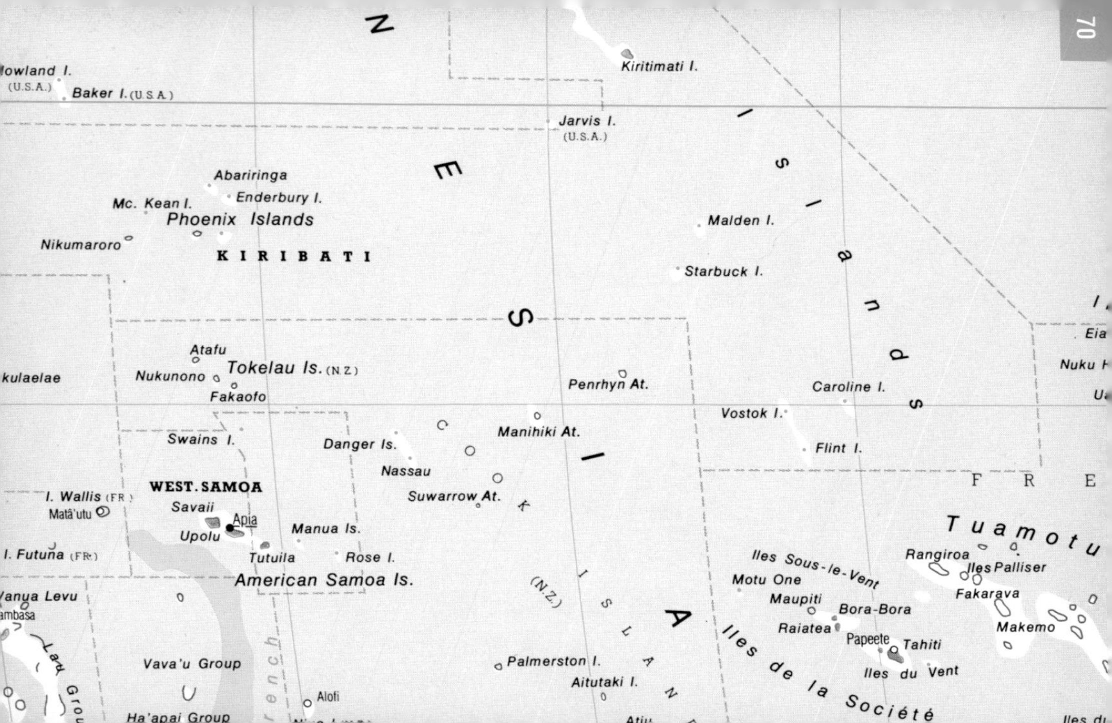
Kiritimati I.
Baker I. (U.S.A.)
(U.S.A.)
Jarvis I.
(U.S.A.)
Abariringa
Enderbury I.
Mc. Kean I.
Phoenix Islands
Nikumaroro
KIRIBATI
Malden I.
Starbuck I.
Islands
Atafu
Tokelau Is. (N.Z.)
Nukunono
Fakaofo
kulaelae
Penrhyn At.
Caroline I.
Eia
Vostok I.
Manihiki At.
Flint I.
Swains I.
Danger Is.
Nassau
WEST. SAMOA
I. Wallis (FR.)
Matâ'utu
Savaii
Apia
Upolu
Suwarrow At.
Manua Is.
Tutuila
Rose I.
I. Futuna (FR.)
American Samoa Is.
(N.Z.)
Tuamotu
Rangiroa
Iles Palliser
Iles Sous-le-Vent
Motu One
Fakarava
Maupiti
Bora-Bora
Raiatea
Makemo
Papeete
Tahiti
Iles du Vent
Iles de la Société
Vava'u Group
Palmerston I.
Aitutaki I.
Alofi
Ha'apai Group

Tongatapu Group
TONGA
10632
Mangaia
Maria
Rurutu
Tubuai
Raivavae
Iles Australes
Raoul I.
Kermadec Is. (N.Z.)
Macaulay I.
Kermadec Trench
10011
North Island
Auckland
Hamilton
Rotorua
Gisborne
71

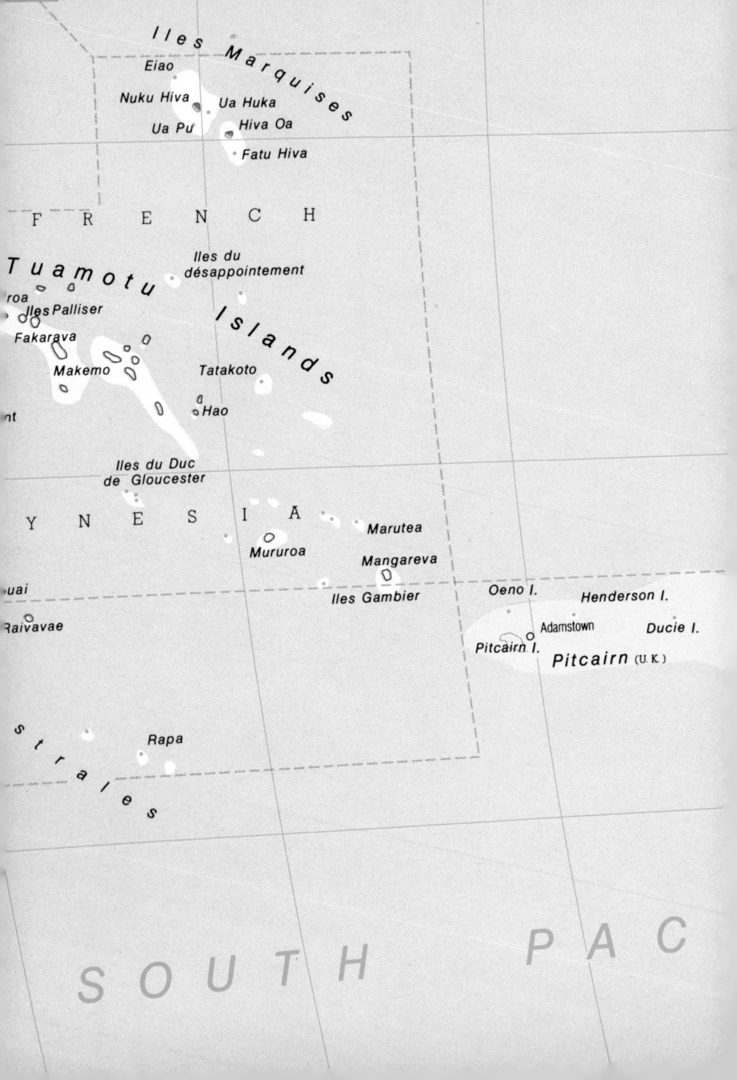

Iles Marquises
Eiao
Nuku Hiva
Ua Huka
Ua Pu
Hiva Oa
Fatu Hiva
F R E N C H
Tuamotu Islands
Iles du désappointement
roa
Iles Palliser
Fakarava
Makemo
Tatakoto
Hao
nt
Iles du Duc de Gloucester
Y N E S I A
Marutea
Mururoa
Mangareva
uai
Iles Gambier
Oeno I.
Henderson I.
Raivavae
Adamstown
Ducie I.
Pitcairn I.
Pitcairn (U.K.)
Rapa
stralés
SOUTH PAC

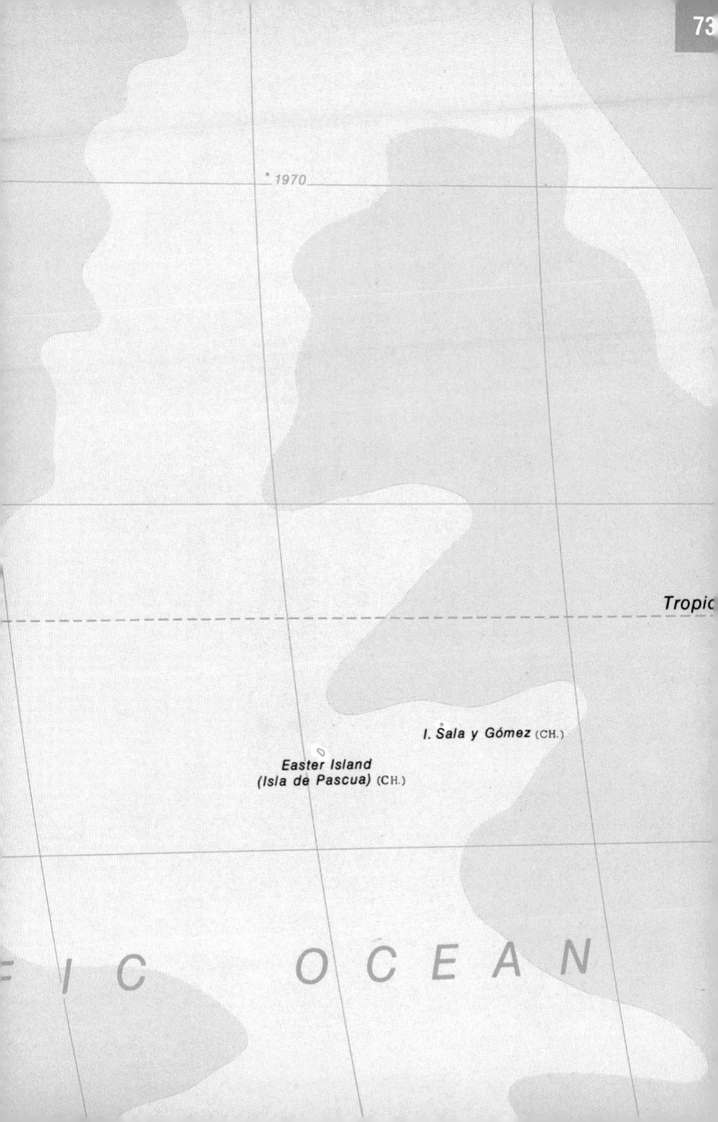

1970
Tropic
I. Sala y Gómez (CH.)
Easter Island
(Isla de Pascua) (CH.)
IC OCEAN

Juneau
Fairbanks
Kotzebue
Bering Strait
ALASKA
U.S.A.
Whitehorse
Yukon
Barrow
O. Vrangel'a
East Siberian Sea
Čerskij
Ust'-Nera
2959
Jakutsk
Lena
Verchojansk
120°
Lensk
Mackenzie
Inuvik
Beaufort Sea
New Siberian Is.
Tiksi
SIBERIA
(Sibir')
Yellowknife
Coppermine
Banks I.
Victoria I.
ARCTIC OCEAN
Laptev Sea
CANADA
Parry Is.
Queen Elizabeth Is.
North Magnetic Pole
North Land
U. S. S. R.
Chesterfield Inlet
Resolute
North Pole
Peary (1909)
Nansen (1895)
Noril'sk
Ellesmere Island
Peary (1906)
Cagni (1900)
Jenisej
Alert
Markham (1876)
Franz Josef Land
Barents (1594)
Kara Sea
80°
Pond Inlet
Qaanaaq
Lockwood (1882)
Baffin Island
Parry (1827)
Baffin Bay
Novaja Zeml'a
Salechard
Iqaluit
Hudson (1607)
Ob'
1883
Ural Mtns.
Svalbard
(NOR.)
Barents Sea
Narian-Mar
70°
GREENLAND
(DEN.)
North Cape
Nuuk (Godthåb)
Hammerfest
Murmansk
Archangel'sk
Syktyvkar
60°
3700
Ammassalik
Norwegian Sea
NORWAY
FIN

Orcadas (ARG.)
Signy (U.K.)
ATLANTIC
South Shetland Is.
Drake Passage
A. Prat (CH.)
Marambio (ARG.)
James Ross I.
Palmer (U.S.A.)
Antarctic Pen.
Weddell Sea
Weddell (1823)
Halley (U.K.)
Coats Land
Rothera (U.K.)
Adelaide I.
Alexander I.
Berkner I.
Filchner Ice Shelf
Edith Ronne Land
4300
Queen Maud Land
+ Cook (1773)
Molod'ožnaja (U.S.S.R.)
Syowa (JAP.)
Enderby Land
INDIAN
Mawson (AUSTR.)
3355
Amery Ice Shelf
80°
Charcot I.
80°
EAST
3950
Ellsworth Land
5140
Vinson Massif
Bellingshausen Sea
South Pole
Amundsen 2800
(14.12.1911)
Amundsen-Scott (U.S.A.)
Scott (18.01.1912)
ANTARCTICA
(U.S.S.R.)
Mirnyj
Transantarctica
(1989-1990)
Queen Mary Coast
Vostok (U.S.S.R.)
3488
Shackleton (1909)
WEST ANTARCTICA
Thurston I.
Cook (1774) +
Amundsen Sea
Marie Byrd Land
4181
Ross Ice Shelf
80°
Scott (1902)
2854
Wilkes Land
Roosevelt I.
Ross (1840)
McMurdo (U.S.A.)
Scott (N.Z.)
3743 Mt. Erebus
OCEAN
70°
PACIFIC
120°
Ross Sea
120°
Victoria Land
Adélie Coast
Dumont d'Urville (FR.)
South Magnetic Pole
60°
Cape Adare
Antarctic Circle
OCEAN
Balleny Is.

INDEX

A	B	A	B
C	D	C	D

A

A. Prat (CHILE) ANTARCTICA 75C
A. Ringnes I. CANADA 5A
Aasiaat (Egedesminde) GREENLAND 21C
Abaco BAHAMAS 11D 13A
Abadan IRAN 38B
Abaiang At. 62B
Abakan SIBERIA 52B
Abariringa 70C
Aberdeen U.K. 30D 34A
Abéché CHAD 37D 40B
Abha SAUDI ARABIA 38D
Abidjan IVORY COAST 24B 36D
Abilene U.S.A. 10D 12A
Abu Dhabi U.A.E. 39A
Abu Simbel EGYPT 37B 38C
Abuja NIGERIA 37C
Acapulco MEXICO 12A
Accra GHANA 36D
Acinsk SIBERIA 52B
Acklins I. BAHAMAS 13A
Acre BRAZIL 14C
Adak I. ALASKA 50B
Adamstown Pitcairn I. 72D
Adana TURKEY 35D 38A
Addis Ababa ETHIOPIA 38D 41A
Adelaide AUSTRALIA 65C
Adelaide I. ANTARCTICA 75C
Aden YEMEN 38D 41B
Adélie Coast ANTARCTICA 75B
Admiralty Is. 62D
Adriatic Sea 34D 35C
Aegean Sea 32C 35C 38A
Afghanistan 39B
Afognak I. Alaska, U.S.A. 6A
Afyon TURKEY 32C 38A
Agadez NIGER 37C 40A
Agadir MOROCCO 23D 34C 36A
Agalega I. (MAURITIUS) 43B 58D
Agaña 62C
Agartala INDIA 56B
Agra INDIA 56A
Agrihan 62C
Aguascalientes MEXICO 12A
Ahmadabad INDIA 39D 56C
Ahvaz IRAN 38B
Ailinglapalap At. 62B
Aimer INDIA 56A
Ain-Sefra ALGERIA 34C 36B
Aitutaki I. 70B
Ajaccio Corse ITALY 34D
Ajan SIBERIA 48D
Ajanta INDIA 56C
Ajdabiyah LIBYA 35C
Ajmer INDIA 39B
Ajon, O. SIBERIA 49A
Akimiski I. CANADA 8B
Akita JAPAN 55A
Akpatok I. CANADA 9A
Akron U.S.A. 8D 11B
Aksu CHINA 52C
Akt'ubinsk KAZAKHSTAN 33C
Akureyri ICELAND 21B 30A
Al Ain U.A.E. 39A
Al Aqabah JORDAN 35D
Al Bayda LIBYA 35C 37B
Al Fashir SUDAN 37D 38C 40B
Al Fayyum EGYPT 35D 37B 38A
Al Hadithah SAUDI ARABIA 35D
Al Hillah IRAQ 38B
Al Hudaydah YEMEN 38D 41A
Al Isma'ilyah EGYPT 35D 38A
Al Khums LIBYA 34D 37A
Al Kufrah LIBYA 37B
Al Ladhiqiyah SYRIA 35D 38A
Al Mahallah al Kubra EGYPT 37B 38A
Al Mukalla YEMEN 39A 39B 39C
Al Masirah OMAN 39C
Al Minya EGYPT 37B 38A
Al Ubayyid SUDAN 37D 38C
Al Uwaynat LIBYA 37B 38C
Alabama U.S.A. 11C
Alagoas BRAZIL 15D 25C
Alaska Peninsula Alaska, U.S.A. 6A 50A
Alaska Range Alaska, U.S.A. 2D
Alaska U.S.A. 2D 74C
Albania 32C 35C
Albany U.S.A. 9C 11B
Alberta CANADA 7D
Albuquerque U.S.A. 10D
Albury AUSTRALIA 65C 66C
Aldabra I. SEYCHELLES 41D 43B
Aldan SIBERIA 48C 53B
Aldan, River SIBERIA 48D
Aldrich, C. ELLESMERE ISLAND 20C
Aleksandrovsk-Sachalinskij SIBERIA 54A
Aleppo SYRIA 35D 38B
Alert CANADA 20C
Ålesund NORWAY 30B
Aleutian Islands Alaska, U.S.A. 50B
Aleutian Trench 50B
Alexander Arch. 6B
Alexander I. ANTARCTICA 75C
Alexandria EGYPT 37B 38A
Algeria 23D 36B
Algiers ALGERIA 34D 36B
Alicante SPAIN 23D 34C
Alice Springs AUSTRALIA 64B
Allahabad INDIA 56A
Alma-Ata KAZAKHSTAN 52C
Almirante Brown (ARGENTINA) 18D
Alofi 70D
Alps, The 34B
Altai Mts. MONGOLIA 52D
Altay CHINA 52D
Amami O. Sa JAPAN 55D
Amapa BRAZIL 15A
Amarillo U.S.A. 10D
Amazon, River BRAZIL 15A
Amazonas BRAZIL 14B
Amazonia BRAZIL 13D 14B
Ambon INDONESIA 61C
Ambrym VANUATU 63B
American Samoa Is. 70D
Amery Ice Shelf 74B
Amga SIBERIA 48D
Amindivi Is. (INDIA) 39D
Amman JORDAN 35D 38B
Ammassalik GREENLAND 21C 74D
Amritsar INDIA 39B 56A
Amsterdam NETHERLANDS 30D 34B
Amsterdam, I. 59B
Amudarja, River TURKMEN REP. 33D
Amundsen G 3D 4C
Amundsen Sea 75D
Amundsen-Scott (U.S.A.) ANTARCTICA 74D
Amur, River SIBERIA 53B
An Nafud SAUDI ARABIA 38B
An'ujskij Chrebet SIBERIA. 49A
Anadyr 49B
Anadyr', River SIBERIA 49B
Anadyrskij Zaliv 49B
Anaheim U.S.A. 10C
Anchorage Alaska, U.S.A. 6B
Anda CHINA 54D
Andaman Is. (INDIA) 56D 60A
Andaman Sea 57C 60A
Andes see Cordillera de los Andes
Andhra Pradesh INDIA 56C
Andizan UZBEKISTAN 33D 52C
Andorra 34C
Andreanof Islands Alaska, U.S.A. 50B
Andros, I. BAHAMAS 11D
Angara, River SIBERIA 52B
Angarsk SIBERIA 53A
Angola 40D 42A
Anguilla (UNITED KINDOM) 13B
Anhwei CHINA 55D 57B
Aniva, M. SIBERIA 54B
Ankang CHINA 57A
Ankara TURKEY 35D
Annaba ALGERIA 34D 37A
Annapolis U.S.A. 11D
Anshan CHINA 55C
Antalya TURKEY 35D 37B 38A
Antananarivo MADAGASCAR 41D 43B
Antarctic Pen. ANTARCTICA 75C
Antarctica Pen. 18D
Anticosti I. CANADA 9D
Antigua and Barbuda 13B
Antilles 13B
Antipodes Is. N.Z. 67A
Antofagasta CHILE 16A
Antsirabé MADAGASCAR 43D
Antsiranana MADAGASCAR 41D 43B
Antwerpen BELGIUM 30D 34B
Anyang CHINA 53D 57B
Apia WEST SAMOA 70D
Apôtres, I. des (FRANCE) 45A
Appalachian Mts. U.S.A. 8D 11D
Arabian Sea 39D
Aracaju BRAZIL 15D 25C
Arafura Sea 61D
Araguaia, River BRAZIL 15C
Aral Sea 33C
Aral'sk KAZAKHSTAN 33D
Archangel'sk RUSSIA 74B
Arctic Ocean 28A 28B 74A 74B
Arequipa PERU 14C 16A
Argentina 16D
Ari Atoll 58C

Arica CHILE 14C 16A
Arizona U.S.A. 10D
Arkalyk KAZAKHSTAN 33D
Arkansas U.S.A. 11C
Arkticeskogo, Instituta O-va SIBERIA 46A
Armenia 32D
Armidale AUSTRALIA 65D 66C
Arnhem Land AUSTRALIA 61D 64B
Arno At. 62B
Arturo Prat (CHILE) 18D
Aru, Kep INDONESIA 61D
Arunachal Pradesh INDIA 56B
Arusha TANZANIA 41C 43A
As Sahra al Libiyah 37B
Asahikawa JAPAN 54B
Asansol INDIA 56B
Ascension (U.K.) 25A
Aschabad TURKMEN REP. 33C 39A
Aseb ETHIOPIA 38D 41A
Asmera ETHIOPIA 38D 41A
Assam INDIA 56B
Astrachan' 33C
Asunción PARAGUAY 16B
Aswan EGYPT 38A
At Ta'if SAUDI ARABIA 38D
Atâr MAURITANIA 24A 36C
Atbarah SUDAN 38C
Atbasar KAZAKHSTAN 33B
Athabasca, L. CANADA 7B 8A
Athabasca, River CANADA 7B
Athens GREECE 32C 35C 38A
Atiu, Cook Is. 70B
Atka I. Alaska, U.S.A. 50B
Atlanta U.S.A. 11D
Atlantic City U.S.A. 9C 11B
Atlantic Ocean 75C 75C
Atlas Mountains ALGERIA & MOROCCO 36B
Attu I. Alaska, U.S.A. 50D
Atufa 70C
Auckland Is. N.Z. 67C
Auckland N.Z. 66B 71D
Augusta AUSTRALIA 64C
Augusta U.S.A. 9C
Aurangabad INDIA 56C
Austin U.S.A. 12A
Australes, Iles 71A
Australia 64B
Austria 31C 34B
Avarua, Cook Is. 71A
Axel Heiberg I. CANADA 5A
Ayers Rock AUSTRALIA 64B
Azores (PORTUGAL) 23D
Azovskoje More U.S.S.R. 32D 35B

B

Babelthuap I. 61B
Babuyan Is. PHILIPPINES 61A
Bacolod PHILIPPINES 61A
Badajoz SPAIN 23D 34C
Baffin Bay 5D 74D
Baffin Island CANADA 5C 74D
Bagdarin SIBERIA 53A
Bagé BRAZIL 17A
Baghdad IRAQ 38B
Baguio PHILIPPINES 57D 61A
Bahama, Grd. BAHAMAS 11D 13A
Bahamas (U.K.) 11D 13A
Bahia Blanca ARGENTINA 16D
Bahia BRAZIL 15D
Bahia de Campeche 12B
Bahia Grande 18A
Bahrain 39A
Baicheng CHINA 53D 54D
Baie-Comeau CANADA 9C
Bairiki Abaing At. 62B
Baja California MEXICO 10C
Bajdarackaja G. 46C
Bajkit SIBERIA 52B
Bajkonur KAZAKHSTAN 33D
Baker I. (U.S.A.) 70C
Baker L. CANADA 4D
Bakersfield U.S.A. 10C
Bakhtaran IRAN 38B
Baku AZERBAIJAN 33C
Balabac Strait 57D 61A
Balagansk SIBERIA 53A
Balchas KAZAKHSTAN 52C
Baleares, Is. SPAIN 34D
Bali INDONESIA 60D
Ballarat AUSTRALIA 65C 66C
Balleny Is. ANTARCTICA 75B
Baltic Sea 31C
Baltic Sea 35A
Baltimore U.S.A. 8D 11B
Bam IRAN 39A
Bamako MALI 24B 36C
Bambari C.A.R. 37D 40B
Bamenda CAMEROON 40A
Bamian AFGHANISTAN 39B
Banda Aceh INDONESIA 60A
Banda Sea 61C
Bandar Seri Begawan BRUNEI 60B
Bandar-e 'Abbas IRAN 39A
Bandung INDONESIA 60D
Banff CANADA 7D
Bangalore INDIA 56C
Bangassou C.A.R. 37D 40B
Bangka INDONESIA 60D
Bangkok THAILAND 57C 60A
Bangladesh 56B
Bangui C.A.R. 37C 40B
Banjarmasin INDONESIA 60D
Banjul GAMBIA 24A 36C
Banks I. CANADA 4A 74C
Banks Is. VANUATU 63A
Baoding CHINA 53D
Barbados 13D
Barcaldine AUSTRALIA 63D 65A
Barcelona SPAIN 34D
Barcelona VENEZUELA 13D
Bareilly INDIA 56A
Barents Sea 29C 74B
Barnaul U.S.S.R. 52A
Barquisimeto VENEZUELA 13C 14A
Barranquilla COLOMBIA 13C 14A
Barrow Alaska, U.S.A. 3A 74C
Basankusu ZAIRE 40B
Basel SWITZERLAND 31C 34B
Basra IRAQ 38B
Bass Strait 65C 66D
Bassas da India (FRANCE) 43C
Bassein BURMA 56D 60A
Basseterre St. CHRISTOPHER AND NEVIS 13B
Bata EQUATORIAL GUINEA 40A
Batan I. PHILIPPINES 61A
Batangas PHILIPPINES 57D 61A
Batdâmbâng KAMPUCHEA 60A
Bathurst I. AUSTRALIA 61D 64B
Bathurst I. CANADA 4B
Bathurst Inlet CANADA 4C
Bathurst, C CANADA 3D
Baton Rouge U.S.A. 12B
Batterbee, C. ANTARCTICA 44D
Batumi GEORGIA 32D 35D
Baubau INDONESIA 61C
Bauchi NIGERIA 37C
Bauru BRAZIL 15C
Beaufort Sea 3B 74C
Beaumont U.S.A. 11C 12B
Beijing see Peking
Beira MOZAMBIQUE 41C 43A
Beirut LEBANON 35D
38A
Bejaïa ALGERIA 34D 36B
Bel'kovskij, O. SIBERIA 47B
Belaja Gora SIBERIA 48B
Belaja Zeml'a, O-va FRANZ JOSEF LAND 29B
Belcher Channel 5A
Belcher I. CANADA 9A
Belet Huen SOMALIA 41B
Belém BRAZIL 15A
Belfast U.K. 23B 30D 34A
Belgium 30D
Belgrade YUGOSLAVIA 32C 35C
Belitung INDONESIA 60D
Belize 12D
Belize City BELIZE 12D
Bella Coola CANADA 7C
Bellinghausen 18D
Bellinghausen Sea 75C
Belmopan BELIZE 12D
Belo Horizonte BRAZIL 15C 17A
Belyj, O. SIBERIA 46C
Benares INDIA 56B
Bendingo AUSTRALIA 65C
Bengal, Bay of 56D
Benghazi LIBYA 35C 37A
Bengkulu INDONESIA 60D
Beni, River BOLIVIA 14D
Benin 36D
Benin City NIGERIA 36D 40A
Benue, River NIGERIA 37C 40A
Berbera SOMALIA 38D 41B
Berbérati C.A.R. 37C 40B
Bereznik RUSSIA 32B
Berezniki SIBERIA 33A
Bergen NORWAY 30B
Bering Sea 50C
Bering Strait 2A 74C
Beringa, O. SIBERIA 49D 50D
Berkner I. ANTARCTICA 75C
Berlin GERMANY 31C 34B
Bermuda Is. (U.K.) 13B
Bern SWITZERLAND 31C 34B
Bernardo O'Higgins (CHILE) 18D
Bethel Alaska, U.S.A. 2C 6A
Béchar ALGERIA 23D 34C 36B
Bharat INDIA 56C
Bhopal INDIA 56A
Bhubaneshwar INDIA 56D
Bhutan 56B
Bialystok POLAND 32A 35A
Biarritz FRANCE 23B 34C
Bihar INDIA 56B
Bijsk SIBERIA 52B

INDEX

ABAB
CDCD

Bikaner INDIA 39B 56A
Bikini Atoll 62A
Bilbao SPAIN 23B 34C
Bilibino SIBERIA 49A
Billings U.S.A. 7D 10B
Bioko I. CAMEROON 37C
Birao C.A.R. 40B
Birjand IRAN 39A
Birmingham U.K. 23B 30D 34A
Biscay, Bay of 23B 34A 34C
Biskra ALGERIA 34D
Bismarck Arch 63C
Bismarck Sea 63C
Bismarck U.S.A. 7D 8C 11A
Bissau GUINEA-BISSAU 24B 36C
Bizerte TUNISIA 34D 37A
Bjørnøya NORWAY 28D
Black Sea 32D 35D
Blagovescensk SIBERIA 54C
Blantyre MALAWI 41C 43A
Blida ALGERIA 34D 36B
Bloemfontein S.A. 42D
Blue Nile, River SUDAN 38C 41A
Bluefields NICARAGUA 12D
Bo SIERRA LEONE 24B 36C
Boa Vista BRAZIL 13D 14B
Boa Vista CAPE VERDE 24C
Bobo-Dioulasso BURKINA FASO 24B 36D
Bodajbo SIBERIA 48C 53A
Bodø NORWAY 31A 74B 28D
Boende ZAIRE 40B
Bogotá COLOMBIA 13C 14A
Boise U.S.A. 10A
Bol'sevik. O. SIBERIA 46B
Bol'soj L'achovskij SIBERIA 48A
Bol. Begicev, O. SIBERIA 47A
Bolivia 14D 16B
Bombay INDIA 39D 56C
Bongor CHAD 40A 37C
Bonin Is. JAPAN 55B
Bonin Trench 55B
Bonn GERMANY 31C 34B
Boothia Pen. CANADA 4D
Bora-Bora Iles de la Société 70B
Bordeaux FRANCE 23B 34C
Borden I. CANADA 4B
Borneo 60D
Bornholm SWEDEN 31C 34B
Borobudur INDONESIA 60D
Borz'a SIBERIA 53B
Bosaso SOMALIA 39C 41B
Boston U.S.A. 9C
Botswana 42D
Bouaké IVORY COAST 24B 36D
Bouar C.A.R. 37C 40A
Bougainville I. P.N.G. 63A
Bounty Is. N.Z. 67A
Bourke AUSTRALIA 65C 66C
Bozeman U.S.A. 7D 10B
Br'ansk RUSSIA 31D 32B 35B
Brahmaputra, River INDIA 56B
Branco, River BRAZIL 13D 14B
Brandon CANADA 8C 11A
Bransfield Strait 18D
Brasília BRAZIL 15C 17A
Brasov ROMANIA 32C 35A
Bratislava CZECHOSLO-VAKIA 31C 35A
Bratsk SIBERIA 52B
Brazil 15C 17A
Brazzaville CONGO 40C 42A
Bremen GERMANY 34B
Brest FRANCE 23B 30D 34A
Brest BYELORUSSIA 31D 32C 35A
Bridgetown BARBADOS 13D
Brisbane AUSTRALIA 65D
Bristol Bay 6A 50A
British Columbia CANADA 7C
Brock I. CANADA 4B
Brodeur Pen .CANADA 5C
Broken Hill AUSTRALIA 65C 66C
Brooks Range Alaska, U.S.A. 2B
Broome AUSTRALIA 64B
Brownsville U.S.A 12A 10D
Brunei 60B
Brussels BELGIUM 30D 34B
Bucaramanga COLOMBIA 13C 14A
Buchara UZBEKISTAN 33D
Bucharest ROMANIA 32C 35C
Budapest HUNGARY 32C 35A
Buenaventura COLOMBIA 14A
Buenos Aires ARGENTINA 16D
Buffalo U.S.A. 8D 11B
Bujumbura BURUNDI 42B
Bukavu ZAIRE 40D 42B
Bulawayo ZIMBABWE 42D
Bulgaria 32C 35C
Buntok INDONESIA 60D
Buor-Chaja, G. 47B
Buraydan SAUDI ARABIA 38B
Burgas BULGARIA 32C 35C
Burkina Faso 24B 36D
Burma 56D 60A
Bursa TURKEY 32C 35C 38A
Buru INDONESIA 61C
Burundi 40D 42B
Bushehr IRAN 39A
Buta ZAIRE 37D 40B
Butaritari At. 62B
Butembo ZAIRE 40B
Buton INDONESIA 61C
Butte U.S.A. 7D 10B
Büdapest HUNGARY 31C
Byam Martin I. CANADA 4B
Byelorussia 31D 32A 35A
Bylot I. CANADA 5C

C

Cabinda ANGOLA 40C 42A
Cabo S. Lucas MEXICO 10C
Cáceres BRAZIL 14D 16B
Cádiz SPAIN 23D 34C
Cagliari Sardegna, ITALY 34D
Cairns AUSTRALIA 63D 65A
Cairo EGYPT 35D 37B 38A
Cajamarca PERU 14C
Calais FRANCE 30D 34A
Calbayog PHILIPPINES 61A
Calcutta INDIA 56D
Calgary CANADA 7D
Cali COLOMBIA 13C 14A
California U.S.A 10A
Callao PERU 14C
Camaguey CUBA 13A
Cambodia see KAMPUCHEA
Cambridge Bay CANADA 4C
Cameroon 37C 40A
Cameroon, Mt. CAMEROON 37C 40A
Campbell I. N.Z. 67D
Campina Grande BRAZIL 15D 25C
Campinas BRAZIL 15C 17A
Campo Grande BRAZIL 15C 17A
Campos BRAZIL 15D 17B
Can Tho VIETNAM 57C 60B
Canada 8A 74C
Canary Islands 23C 36A
Canaveral, C. U.S.A. 11D 13A
Canberra AUSTRALIA 65C 66C
Cancún MEXICO 12B
Candlemas I. 19B
Canton CHINA 55D 57B
Cape Adare ANTARCTICA 75B
Cape Barren I. AUSTRALIA 66D
Cape Breton I. CANADA 9D
Cape Horn (Cabo de Hornos) 18B
Cape of Good Hope S.A. 27D 42C
Cape Town S.A. 27D 42C
Cape Verde 24C
Cape York Peninsula AUSTRALIA 63C 65A
Caracas VENEZUELA 13C 14B
Caravelas BRAZIL 15D 17B 25D
Cardiff U.K. 23B 30D 34A
Cargados Carajos Shoals (MAURITIUS) 58D
Caribbean Sea 13C
Carnarvon AUSTRALIA 64A
Caroline I. 70A
Caroline Islands 62D
Carpathians ROMANIA 31D 35A
Carpentaria, Gulf of 63C 65A
Carson City U.S.A. 10A
Cartagena COLOMBIA 13C
Cartwright CANADA 9B
Casablanca MOROCCO 23D 34C

36A
Casper U.S.A. 10B
Caspian Sea 33C
Castries SAINT LUCIA 13D
Cat. I. BAHAMAS 11D
13A
Catamarca ARGENTINA
16B
Catania Sicilia, ITALY 34D
37A
Catoche C. MEXICO 12B
Caucasus 32D
Caxias do Sul BRAZIL 17A
Cayenne GUYANE 15A
Cayman Is. (U.K.) 12B
Ceará BRAZIL 15B
Cebu PHILIPPINES 61A
Ceboskory RUSSIA 32B
Cedros, I. MEXICO 10C
Cel'abinsk SIBERIA 33A
Celebes INDONESIA 61C
Celebes Sea 61C
Celinograd KAZAKHSTAN
33B
52C
Central African Republic
37D
Central Siberian Plateau
47C
Cerepovec RUSSIA 32A
Cerkassy UKRAINE 31D
32C
35B
Cernigov UKRAINE 31D
32C
35B
Cernovcy UKRAINE 32C
Cerskij SIBERIA 49A
74A
Cesskaja Guba 29D
Ceuta (SPAIN) 23D
34C
36B
Ceylon see Sri Lanka
Chabarovsk SIBERIA 54D
Chaco ARGENTINA 16B
Chad 37C
40B
Chad, Lake CHAD 37C
40A
Chagos Archipelago (U.K.)
58D
Chal'mer-Ju RUSSIA 46C
Chandigarh INDIA 56A
Chandyga SIBERIA 48D
Changchun CHINA 54D
Channel-Port aux Basques
CANADA 9D
Chansha CHINA 57B
Chanty-Mansijsk SIBERIA
33B
Char'kov UKRAINE 32D
35B
Charcot I. ANTARCTICA
75C
Chari, River CHAD 37C
40B
Charleston U.S.A. 11D
13A
Charleville AUSTRALIA 63D
65A
Charlotte U.S.A. 11D
Charlottetown CANADA
9C
Chatanga SIBERIA 47A
Chatangskij Zaliv. 47A
Chatham I. N.Z. 67A
Chattanooga U.S.A. 11D
Cheju-do SOUTH KOREA
55C
Chekiang CHINA 55D
57B
Chengde CHINA 53D
55C
Chengdu CHINA 57A
Cherson UKRAINE 31D
32D
35B
Chesterfield Inlet CANADA
74C
Chesterfield, Iles
(FRANCE) 63B
65B
Chetumal MEXICO 12B
Cheyenne U.S.A. 10B
Chiang Mai THAILAND 57C
60A
Chibougamau CANADA 9C
Chicago U.S.A. 11A
Chichen Itzá MEXICO 12B
Chiclayo PERU 14C
Chicoutimi CANADA 9C
Chidley, C. CANADA 9B
Chihuahua MEXICO 10D
Chile 16D
Chillán CHILE 16C
Chiloé, I. de CHILE 16C
Chimborazo ECUADOR 14A
13C
China 53C
54D
56B
Chinchilla AUSTRALIA 63D
65D
Chittagong BANGLADESH
56D
Choiseul I. SOLOMON
ISLANDS 63A
Chon Buri THAILAND 57C
60A
Chongqing CHINA 57A
Chonos, Arch. de los
CHILE 16C
18A
Chonuu SIBERIA 48B
Choybalsan MONGOLIA
53D
Chrebet Cerskogo SIBERIA
48B
Christchurch N.Z. 66B
Christmas I. (AUSTRALIA)
60D
Chubut ARGENTINA 16D
Chubut, River ARGENTINA
16D
Chukchi Sea 2A
Churchill CANADA 8B
Cimkent KAZAKHSTAN
33D
Cincinnati U.S.A. 8D
11B
Circle Alaska, U.S.A. 3C
Cita SIBERIA 53A
Ciudad Bolivar
VENEZUELA 13D
14B
Ciudad Guayana
VENEZUELA 13D
14B
Ciudad Juárez MEXICO
10D
12A
Ciudad Victoria MEXICO
10D
12A
Clarence I. 19C
Clarión, I. MEXICO 12C
Clavering Ø GREENLAND
20B
Clermont-Fd. FRANCE 34B
Cleveland U.S.A. 11B
Clipperton, I. (FRANCE)
12C
Cluj-Napoca ROMANIA 31D
32C
35A
Coast Mountains CANADA
7A
7C
Coats I. CANADA 9A
Coburg I. CANADA 5B
Cochabamba BOLIVIA 14D
16B
Cochin INDIA 56C
Cochrane CANADA 8D
11B
Cockburn Town BAHAMAS
13A
Coco, I. del (COSTA RICA)
12D
Cocos. Is. (AUSTRALIA)
60C
Cod, C. U.S.A. 9C
Coëtivy SEYCHELLES 43B
58D
Coimbatore INDIA 56C
Coimbra PORTUGAL 23D
34C
Cologne see Köln
Colombia 13C
14A
Colombo SRI LANKA 56C
58A
Colorado Springs U.S.A.
10B
Colorado U.S.A. 10D
Colorado, River
ARGENTINA 16D
Colorado, River U.S.A. 10D
Columbia U.S.A. 11D
Columbia, River U.S.A. 7C
10A
Columbus, Ohio, U.S.A. 8D
11B
Columbus, Georgia, U.S.A.
11D
Colville, River Alaska,
U.S.A. 2B
Comodoro Rivadavia
ARGENTINA 16D
18A
Comorin. C. INDIA 56C
Comoros 41D
43A
Con Son VIETNAM 57C
60B
Conakry GUINEA 24B
36C
Concepción CHILE 16C
Concepción PARAGUAY
14D
16B
Concord U.S.A. 9C
Congo 40C
42A
Congo, River CONGO 40B
42A
Connecticut U.S.A. 9C
Constanta ROMANIA 32C
35C
Constantine ALGERIA 36B
Cook Inlet 2D
6B
Cook Islands 70B
Cook, Mt. N.Z. 66B
Cooktown AUSTRALIA 63C
65A
Coolgardie AUSTRALIA 64C
Copenhagen DENMARK
31C
34B
Copiapó CHILE 16A
Coppermine CANADA 4C
74C
Coral Sea 63C
65B
Cordillera de los Andes
PERU 14A
14D
16B
16D
Córdoba ARGENTINA 16B
Córdoba SPAIN 23D
34C
Cork IRELAND 23B
30C
Corner Brook
Newfoundland, CANADA
9D
22A
Cornwall I. CANADA 5A
Cornwallis I. CANADA 5A
Coronation G 4C
Corpus Christi U.S.A. 10D
12A
Corrientes ARGENTINA 16B
Corse FRANCE 34D
Corsica, see Corse
Corumbá BRAZIL 16B
Costa Rica 12D
Crajova ROMANIA 32C
Crescent City U.S.A. 10A
Crete see Kriti
Crusoe, I.R. (Juan
Fernández) 16C
Cruzeirio do Sul BRAZIL
14C
Cuba 13A
Cucuta COLOMBIA 13C
14A
Cuenca ECUADOR 14A
Cuiabá BRAZIL 17A
Cukotskij P-ov SIBERIA 2A
Culiacán MEXICO 10D
12A
Cumaná VENEZUELA 13D
14B
Cumberland Is.
AUSTRALIA 63D
65B
Cumberland Sound 9B
Curaçao (NETHERLANDS)
13C
14B
Curitiba BRAZIL 17A
Cuzco PERU 14C
Cyprus 35D
37B
38A
Cyrenaica LIBYA 35C

INDEX

ABAB
CDCD

37B
Czechoslovakia 34B
Czestochowa POLAND 31C 32C 35A

D

Da Hinggan Ling CHINA 53B 53D 54D
Da Nang VIETNAM 57C 60B
Daito Zima JAPAN 55B
Dakar SENEGAL 24A 36C
Dakhla WESTERN SAHARA 23D 24A 36A
Dal'negorsk SIBERIA 54D
Dal'nerecensk SIBERIA 54D
Dalandzadgad MONGOLIA 53C
Dali CHINA 57A
Dalian CHINA 55C
Dallas U.S.A. 11C
Daloa IVORY COAST 24B
Damascus SYRIA 35D
Damavand IRAN 39A
Dandong CHINA 55C
Danger Is. 70D
Danube, River 32C 35C
Dar es Salaam TANZANIA 41C 43A
Darhan MONGOLIA 53C
Darjeeling INDIA 56B
Darling, River AUSTRALIA 65C 66C
Darnley, C. ANTARCTICA 45C
Darwin AUSTRALIA 61D 64B
Dasht-e-Kavir IRAN 39A
Datong CHINA 53D
Daugava, River LATVIA, BYELORUSSIA, RUSSIA 31D 32A 35A
Daugavpils LATVIA 31D 32A 35A
Davao PHILIPPINES 61A
Davenport U.S.A. 8C 11A
David PANAMA 12D 14A
Davis Strait 5D
Dawson CANADA 3C 7A
Dawson Creek CANADA 7C
Dayr az Zawr SYRIA 38B
Dayton U.S.A. 8D
Daytona Beach U.S.A. 11D 13A
Delaware U.S.A. 11D
Delhi INDIA 56A
Den Haag NETHERLANDS 30D 34B
Denmark 31C 34B
Denmark Strait 21A 30A
Denpasar Bali, INDONESIA 60D
Denver U.S.A. 10B
Des Moines U.S.A. 8C 11A
Dese ETHIOPIA 38D 41A
Deseado, River ARGENTINA 18A
Desolación, I. CHILE 18A
Detroit U.S.A. 8D 11B
Devon I. CANADA 5A
Désappointment, Iles du 72A
Dhaka BANGLADESH 56B
Diamantino BRAZIL 14D
Diego Garcia 58D
Diego Ramirez, Islas (CHILE) 18B
Dijon FRANCE 30D 34B
Dire Dawa ETHIOPIA 38D 41A
Dirk Hartogs I. AUSTRALIA 64A
Disko GREENLAND 21C
Dixon Entrance 6D
Djibouti 38D 41A
Djibouti DJIBOUTI 38D 41A
Dmitrija Lapteva, Pr. 48A
Dnepr, River UKRAINE, BYELORUSSIA, RUSSIA 31D 35A
Dnepropetrovsk UKRAINE 32D 35B
Dnestr, River UKRAINE, MOLDAVIA 31D 32C 35A
Do Sul BRAZIL 15C
Dodge City U.S.A. 10D
Dodoma TANZANIA 41C 43A
Doha QATAR 39A
Dominica 13D
Dominican Republic 13A
Don, River RUSSIA 32D 35B
Doneck UKRAINE 32D 35B
Douala CAMEROON 37C 40A
Dover U.S.A. 8D 11B
Dover U.K. 30D 34A
Drake Passage 18D 75C
Drakensberg Mts. S.A. 42D
Drâa, River MOROCCO 23D 34C 36A
Dresden GERMANY 31C 34B
Dubai U.A.E. 39A
Dubawnt L CANADA 4C
Dubbe AUSTRALIA 65C 66C
Dublin IRELAND 23B
Dubrovnik YUGOSLAVIA 32C 35C
Ducie I. 72D
Dudinka SIBERIA 46D
Duluth U.S.A. 8C 11A
Dumont d'Urville (FRANCE) ANTARCTICA 75B
Dundee U.K. 34A
Dunedin N.Z. 67A
Dunhuang CHINA 52D
Dunqulah SUDAN 37D 38C
Durango MEXICO 10D 12A
Durango U.S.A. 10D
Durban S.A. 42D
Dusanbe TADZHIKISTAN 33D 39B 52C
Düsseldorf GERMANY 31C 34B
Dvina Sev, River RUSSIA 32B
Dzambul KAZAKHSTAN 33D
Dzaoudzi Mayotte (FRANCE) 41D 43B
Dzezkazgan KAZAKHSTAN 33D
Dønna NORWAY 28D 31A

E

East Antarctica 75A
East China Sea 55D
East London S.A. 42D
East Siberian Sea 74A
Easter Island (CHILE) 73C
Eastmain CANADA 9C 11B
Ecuador 13C
Edgeøya (NORWAY) 28A
Edinburgh U.K. 30D 34A
Edith Ronne Land ANTARCTICA 75C
Edmonton CANADA 7D
Éfaté VANUATU 63B
Eglinton I. CANADA 4A
Egypt 37B 38A
Eiao 72A
Ekimcan SIBERIA 54C
El Calafate ARGENTINA 18A
El Paso U.S.A. 10D 12A
El Salvador 12D
El-Oued ALGERIA 34D 37A
El-Goléa ALGERIA 36B
Elazig TURKEY 32D 35D 38B
Elbe, River GERMANY 31C 34B
Elbert, Mt U.S.A 10B
Elephant I. 19C
Eleuthera BAHAMAS 11D 13A
Elgon, Mt. UGANDA 41A
Ellef Ringnes I. CANADA 5A
Ellesmere Island CANADA 5B 74D
Ellsworth Land ANTARCTICA 75C
Emerald I. CANADA 4B
Emi Koussi CHAD 37C
Enderbury I. 70C
Enderby Land ANTARCTICA 44D 75A
Enggano INDONESIA 60C
English Channel 23B 30D 34A
Eniwetok Atoll 62A
Ensenada MEXICO 10C
d'Entrecasteaux Is. P.N.G. 63C
Entre Rios ARGENTINA 16D
Enugu NIGERIA 37C
Epi VANUATU 63B
Erebus, Mt ANTARCTICA 75B
Erenhot CHINA 53D
Erie U.S.A. 8D 11B
Erie, L. CANADA 8D 11B
Erie, L. U.S.A. 8D 11B
Erromango VANUATU 63B
Erzurum TURKEY 32D 35D 38B
Escanaba U.S.A. 8D
Esfahan IRAN 39A
Eskimo Point CANADA 8B
Esmeralda VENEZUELA 13D 14B
Esperanza (ARGENTINA) 19C
Espirito Santo BRAZIL 15D 17B
Espiritu Santo VANUATU 63A
Esquel ARGENTINA 16D
Estados, I. de los ARGENTINA 18B
Estonia 31D 32A
Estreito BRAZIL 15C
Ethiopia 38D 41A
Etna Sicilia ITALY 34D
Eugene U.S.A. 10A
Euphrates, River IRAQ 35D 38B
Eureka U.S.A. 10A
Europa (FRANCE) 43C
Evansville U.S.A. 11C
Everest, Mt. NEPAL 56B
Eyre, L. AUSTRALIA 65C

F

Fada CHAD 37D 40B
Færøerne (DENMARK) 30B

Fairbanks Alaska, U.S.A. 2D 74C
Faisalabad PAKISTAN 39B 56A
Fakaofo 70C
Fakarava 70B 72A
Falkland Islands (Islas Malvinas) (U.K.) 18B
False Pass Alaska, U.S.A. 50A
Faraday (U.K.) 18D
Farewell, C. N.Z. 66B
Fargo U.S.A. 8C 11A
Faroes see Færøerne
Farvel, K. GREENLAND 74D
Fatu Hiva 72A
Faya CHAD 37C
Federated States of Micronesia 62D
Feira de Santana BRAZIL 15D
Fernando de Noronha (BRAZIL) 15B 25C
Fès MOROCCO 23D 34C 36B
Fianarantsoa MADAGASCAR 43D
Fiji 70D
Filchner Ice Shelf ANTARCTICA 75C
Finisterre, C. SPAIN 23B 34C
Finland 28D 31B 32A 74B
Finland, G. of 31B 32A
Firenze ITALY 34D
Flin Flon CANADA 8A
Flinders I. AUSTRALIA 66D
Flint I. 70B
Flint U.S.A. 8D 11B
Florence see Firenze
Flores GUATEMALA 12B
Flores INDONESIA 61C
Flores, I. (PORTUGAL) 22D
Florianópolis BRAZIL 17A
Florida U.S.A. 11D
Florida, Str. of 11D 12B
Fonte Boa BRAZIL 14B
Formosa ARGENTINA 16B
Fort Frances CANADA 8C 11A
Fort Good Hope CANADA 3D
Fort Lauderdale U.S.A. 11D
Fort McMurray CANADA 7B
Fort McPherson CANADA 3C
Fort Nelson CANADA 7A
Fort Providence CANADA 7B
Fort Severn CANADA 8B
Fort Simpson CANADA 3D 7B
Fort Smith CANADA 7B 8A
Fort Worth U.S.A. 11C
Fort Yukon Alaska, U.S.A. 3C
Fort-de-France Martinique (FRANCE) 13D
Fortaleza BRAZIL 15B 25C
Fouta Djalon GUINEA 24B 36C
Fox Islands ALASKA 50B
Foxe Basin 5C
Foz do Iguaçú BRAZIL 17A
France 23B 30D 34A
Franceville GABON 40C 42A
Francistown BOTSWANA 42D
Frankfort U.S.A. 11C
Frankfurt GERMANY 31C 34B
Franz Josef Land 29A 75D
Fraser I. AUSTRALIA 63D 65B
Fredericton CANADA 9C
Frederikshavn DENMARK 31C 34B
Freetown SIERRA LEONE 24B 36C
French Polynesia 70B 72A
Fresno U.S.A. 10C
Frunze KIRGHIZIA 52C
Fuerteventura Canary Islands (SPAIN) 23C 36A
Fujiyama, Mt. JAPAN 55A
Fukien CHINA 55D 57B
Funchal Madeira Islands (PORTUGAL) 23C 36A
Fushun CHINA 54D
Futuna, I. (FRANCE) 70D
Fuzhou CHINA 55D 57B

G

Gabès TUNISIA 34D 37A
Gabon 40A
Gaborone BOTSWANA 42D
Gafsa TUNISIA 34D 37A
Galati ROMANIA 32C 35A
Galápagos Islands (ECUADOR) 12D
Galcaio SOMALIA 38D 41B
Galle SRI LANKA 56C 58A
Gallup U.S.A. 10D
Galveston U.S.A. 11C 12B
Galway IRELAND 23B 30C
Gambela ETHIOPIA 38D 41A
Gambia 24A 36C
Gambier, Iles 72C
Gander Newfoundland, CANADA 9D 22A
Ganges, River INDIA 56A 56B
Ganzhou CHINA 57B
Gao MALI 36D
Gardner Pinnacles Hawaii, U.S.A. 69C
Gardo SOMALIA 41B
Garoua CAMEROON 37C 40A
Garry L. CANADA 4D
Gary U.S.A. 8D 11A
Gaspé CANADA 9C
Gaya INDIA 56B
Gaziantep TURKEY 35D 38B
Gdansk POLAND 31C 35A
Gdynia POLAND 31C 35A
Geelong AUSTRALIA 65C 66D
Gejiu CHINA 57A
General Santos PHILIPPINES 61A
Genève SWITZERLAND 34B
Genova ITALY 34D
George Town MALAYSIA 57C 60A
Georgetown GUYANA 13D 14B
Georgia U.S.A. 11D 12B
Georgia 32D 35D
Geraldton AUSTRALIA 64C
Germany 31C 34B
Ghana 24B 36D
Ghudamis LIBYA 34D 37A
Gibraltar (U.K.) 23D 34C 36B
Gibraltar, Strait of 23D 34C 36A
Gibson Desert AUSTRALIA 64B
Gilbert Islands 62B
Gisborne N.Z. 66B 71D
Giza EGYPT 35D 37B 38A
Glasgow U.K. 30D 34A
Glendive U.S.A. 7D 10B
Gliwice POLAND 35A 31C
Gloucester, Iles du Duc de 70B 72A
Gobabis Namibia S.A. 27B
Gobernado Gregores ARGENTINA 18A
Gobi Desert MONGOLIA 53C
Goiás BRAZIL 15C 17A
Goiânia BRAZIL 15C 17A
Golfo de California 10C
Golmud CHINA 56B
Gomel' BYELORUSSIA 31D 32A 35A
Gonder ETHIOPIA 38D 41A
Goose Bay CANADA 9D
Gora El'brus RUSSIA 32D 35D
Gorakhpur INDIA 56B
Gorgan IRAN 39A
Gorontalo INDONESIA 61C
Gotland SWEDEN 31C 35A
Gough I. (U.K.) 26D
Göteborg SWEDEN 31C 34B
Graham I. CANADA 5A
Gran Canaria Canary Islands (SPAIN) 23C 36A
Granada SPAIN 23D 34C 36B
Grand Canyon U.S.A. 10D
Grand Erg Occidental ALGERIA 34C 36B
Grand Erg Oriental ALGERIA 34D
Grand Junction U.S.A 10B
Grand Rapids CANADA 8A
Grand Rapids U.S.A. 8D 11B
Graz AUSTRIA 31C 34B
Great Australian Bight 64D
Great Barrier Reef AUSTRALIA 63D 65A
Great Basin U.S.A. 10A
Great Bear Lake CANADA 3D
Great Dividing Range AUSTRALIA 63D 65A 65C 66C
Great Falls U.S.A. 7D 10B
Great Salt Lake U.S.A. 10B
Great Sandy Desert AUSTRALIA 64B
Great Slave Lake CANADA 7B
Great Victoria Desert AUSTRALIA 64D
Greater Antilles 13A
Greece 35C
Greem-Bell, O FRANZ JOSEF LAND 29B
Green Bay U.S.A. 8D 11A
Greenland (DENMARK) 20B 20D 74D
Greensboro U.S.A. 11D
Grenada 13D
Grodno BYELORUSSIA 31D 32A
Groningen NETHERLANDS

30D
Groote Eylandt AUSTRALIA 65A
Grosnyj RUSSIA 32D
Guadalajara MEXICO 12A
Guadalcanal SOLOMON ISLANDS 63A
Guadalupe, I. de (MEXICO) 10C
Guadeloupe (FRANCE) 13D
Guam (U.S.A.) 62C
Guan Xian CHINA 57A
Guanajoato MEXICO 12A
Guaporé, River BRAZIL, BOLIVIA 14D
Guatemala 12D
Guatemala GUATEMALA 12D
Guaviare, River COLOMBIA 13C 14B
Guayaquil ECUADOR 14A
Guaymas MEXICO 10D
Guilin CHINA 57A
Guinea 24B 36C
Guinea-Bissau 36C
Guiyang CHINA 57A
Gujarat INDIA 39B 56A
Gujranwala PAKISTAN 39B 56A
Gulf of Aden 41B
Gulf of Alaska 6B
Gulf of Boothia 4D
Gulf of Bothnia 32A
Gulf of Guinea 36D
Gulf of Mexico 11C 12B
Gulf of Oman 39A
Gulf of Thailand 57C 60A
Gulf, The 39A
Gulf of Tonkin 57C 60B
Gulu UGANDA 37D 41A
Gunnbjørns Fjeld GREENLAND 21A
Guntur INDIA 56C
Gurjev KAZAKHSTAN 33C
Guwahati INDIA 56B
Guyana 13D 14B
Guyane 15A
Gwalior INDIA 56A
Gweru ZIMBABWE 42B

H

Ha'apai Group 70D
Hague, The see Den Haag
Ha'il SAUDI ARABIA 38B
Haifa ISRAEL 35D 38A
Haikou CHINA 57D 60B
Hailar CHINA 53B
Hainan Dao CHINA 57D 60B
Haiphong VIETNAM 57C 60B
Haiti 13A
Hakodate JAPAN 54B
Halifax CANADA 9C
Hall Is. 62D
Halley (U.K.) 75C
Halmahera INDONESIA 61D
Hamada du Drâa ALGERIA 23D 34C 36B
Hamadan IRAN 38B
Hamburg GERMANY 31C 34B
Hamersley Ra. AUSTRALIA 64A
Hami CHINA 52D
Hamilton Bermuda Is (U.K.) 13B
Hamilton N.Z. 66B 71D
Hammerfest NORWAY 28D 31A 74B
Hangzhou CHINA 55D 57B
Hannover GERMANY 31C 34B
Hanoi VIETNAM 57C 60B
Harare ZIMBABWE 42B
Harbin CHINA 54D
Hargeysa SOMALIA 38D 41B
Harper LIBERIA 24B 36C
Harrington-Harbour CANADA 9D
Harrisburg U.S.A. 8D 11B
Hartford U.S.A. 9C
Haryana INDIA 39B 56A
Hassi-Messaoud ALGERIA 34D 36B
Hatinohe JAPAN 55A
Hatizyo Za JAPAN 55A
Hatteras, C. U.S.A. 11D
Havana CUBA 11D 12B
Havre St. Pierre CANADA 9C
Havre U.S.A. 7D 10B
Hawaii Hawaii (U.S.A.) 69A
Hay AUSTRALIA 65C 66C
Hay River CANADA 7B
Hazen Strait 4B
Heard Island (AUSTRALIA) 45B
Hebrides U.K. 30D 34A
Hebron CANADA 9B
Hecate Str. 7C
Hechuan CHINA 57A
Hefei CHINA 55D 57B
Hegang CHINA 54D
Heilong Jiang, River CHINA 53B
Heilungkiang CHINA 54D
Helena U.S.A 7D 10B
Helsinki FINLAND 31B 32A
Henderson I. 72D
Hengyang CHINA 57B
Heraklion see Iráklio
Herat AFGHANISTAN 39A
Hermosillo MEXICO 10D
High Level CANADA 7B
Hilo Hawaii, U.S.A. 69A
Himachal Pradesh INDIA 56A
Himalayas 56B
Hirosaki JAPAN 55A
Hiroshima JAPAN 55C
Hitra NORWAY 31A
Hiva Oa 72A
Ho Chi Minh City VIETNAM 57C 60B
Hobart Tasmania, AUSTRALIA 66D
Hohhot CHINA 53D
Hokkaido JAPAN 54B
Holguin CUBA 13A
Homer Alaska, U.S.A. 2D 6B
Homs SYRIA 35D 38B
Honan CHINA 57B
Honduras 12D
Honduras, G. of 12B
Hong Kong (U.K.) 55D 57D
Honiara SOLOMON ISLANDS 63A
Honolulu Hawaii, U.S.A. 69A
Honsyu JAPAN 55A
Hopeh CHINA 53D
Hoste, I. CHILE 18A
Hotan CHINA 56A
Houlton U.S.A. 9C
Houston U.S.A. 11C 12A
Hovgaards Ø GREENLAND 20B
Howe, C. AUSTRALIA 65C 66D
Howland I. (U.S.A.) 70C
Huainan CHINA 55C 57B
Huambo ANGOLA 40C 42A
Huang He, River CHINA 57A
Huascarán PERU 14C
Hubli INDIA 56C
Hudson Bay 8B
Hudson Str. 9A
Hue VIETNAM 57C 60B
Hukuoka JAPAN 55C
Humaitá BRAZIL 14D
Hungary 31C 32C 35A
Hungnam NORTH KOREA 55C
Huntsville U.S.A. 11C
Huon, I. 63B
Huron, L. CANADA 8D 11B
Huron, L. U.S.A. 8D 11B
Hyderabad INDIA 56C
Hyderabad PAKISTAN 39B

I

Iasi ROMANIA 31D 32C 35A
Ibadan NIGERIA 36D 40A
Ibagué COLOMBIA 13C 14A
Ibiza SPAIN 34C
Ice Shelf Larsen 18D
Iceland 21B 30A 74D
Idaho U.S.A. 10B
Ifalik At. 62D
Igarka SIBERIA 46D
Iguaçú Falls BRAZIL 17A
Ihavandiffulu At. MALDIVES 39D 58C
Ikela ZAIRE 40B
Il'pyrskij SIBERIA 49D
Iles Crozet (FRANCE) 45A
Iles Loyauté 63B
Ilhas Martim Vaz (BRAZIL) 25D 26A
Ilhéus BRAZIL 15D 25D
Illimani BOLIVIA 14D 16B
Illinois U.S.A. 8C 11A
Iloilo PHILIPPINES 61A
Ilulissat (Jakobshavn) GREENLAND 21C
Imperatriz BRAZIL 15A
Imphal INDIA 56B
In Salah ALGERIA 36B
Inagua, I. BAHAMAS 13A
Inari FINLAND 29C 31B
Independence Fj. GREENLAND 20A
India 56C
Indian Ocean 75A 75B
Indiana U.S.A. 8D 11B
Indigirka, River SIBERIA 48B
Indonesia 60D 61C
Indore INDIA 56C
Indus, River PAKISTAN 39B
Inhambane MOZAMBIQUE 43C
Inner Mongolia CHINA 53D
Innsbruck AUSTRIA 31C 34B
Inuvik CANADA 3D 74C
Invercargill N.Z. 67A
Inverness U.K. 30D 34A
Ionian Sea 35C 37A
Iowa U.S.A. 8C
Ipoh MALAYSIA 60A
Ipswich AUSTRALIA 65D 66C
Iqaluit CANADA 9B 74D
Iquique CHILE 14C 16A
Iquitos PERU 14A
Iráklio GREECE 35C 37B
Iran 39A
Iraq 35D

38B
Ireland 23B
30C
Irkutsk SIBERIA 53A
Irtys, River 52C
33B
Isabela, I., Galápagos
Islands 12D
Isafjördur ICELAND 21A
30A
Islamabad PAKISTAN 39B
56A
Islas Juan Fernández
(CHILE) 16C
Israel 35D
38A
Istanbul TURKEY 32C
35C
Italy 34D
Itanagar INDIA 56B
Ittoqqortoormiit
(Scoresbysund)
GREENLAND 21A
30A
Iturup, O. 54B
Ivalo FINLAND 29C
31B
Ivanovo RUSSIA 32B
35B
Ivdel' SIBERIA 33A
Ivory Coast 24B
36D
Izevsk RUSSIA 33A
Izmir TURKEY 32C
35C
38A
Izu Trench 55B

J

Jabalpur INDIA 56A
Jackson U.S.A. 11C
Jacksonsville U.S.A. 13A
11D
Jaffna SRI LANKA 56C
Jaipur INDIA 56A
Jakarta INDONESIA 60D
Jakutsk SIBERIA 48C
74A
Jalta CRIMEA 32D
35D
Jaluit At. 62B
Jamaica 13A
Jambi INDONESIA 60D
James Bay 8B
James Ross I.
ANTARCTICA 19C
75C
Jammu and Kashmir INDIA
56A
Jammu Kashmir INDIA 56A
Jan Mayen (NORWAY) 30B
Jana, River SIBERIA 48A
Japan 55A
Japan, Sea of 55A
55C
Japan Trench 55A
Japurá, River BRAZIL 14B
Jaroslavl' RUSSIA 32B
35B
Jarvis I. (U.S.A.) 70A
Jason Pen. 18D
Jasper CANADA 7C
Java INDONESIA 60D
Java Trench 60D
Jayapura INDONESIA 61D
62D
Jeddah SAUDI ARABIA 38D
Jefferson City U.S.A. 8C
11A
Jelizavety, M. SIBERIA 54C
Jenisej, River SIBERIA 46D
52B
74B
Jenisejsk SIBERIA 52B
Jeniseskij Zaliv 46C
Jerba, I. de TUNISIA 34D
37A
Jerevan ARMENIA 32D
Jerusalem 35D
38A
Jiamusi CHINA 54D
Jilin CHINA 54D
Jinan CHINA 53D
Jingdezhen CHINA 55D
57B
Jining CHINA 53D
55C
57B
Jinsha, River CHINA 57A
Jinzhou CHINA 53D
Jiujiang CHINA 55D
57B
Jixi CHINA 54D
João Pessoa BRAZIL 15D
25C
Jodhpur INDIA 39B
56A
Joensuu FINLAND 31B
32A
Johannesburg S.A. 42D
Johnston I. (U.S.A.) 69C
Johor Bahru MALAYSIA
60D
Joinville BRAZIL 17A
Jones Sound 5A
Jordan 35D
Jotunheimen NORWAY 31A
Jönkoping SWEDEN 31C
34B
Juan de Nova (FRANCE)
41C
Juazeiro BRAZIL 15D
Juazeiro do Norte BRAZIL
15D
Juba SUDAN 37D
41A
Juiz de Fora BRAZIL 15C
17A
Jujuy ARGENTINA 16B
Juneau Alaska, U.S.A. 7A
74C
Juruá, River BRAZIL 14C
Juruena, River BRAZIL 14D
Juzno-Sachalinsk SIBERIA
54B

K

K'achta SIBERIA 53A
Kabul AFGHANISTAN 39B
Kabwe ZAMBIA 40D
42B
Kaduna NIGERIA 37C
Kaesong NORTH KOREA
55C
Kaitaia N.Z. 66A
Kalahari Desert
BOTSWANA 42D
Kalemie ZAIRE 40D
42B
Kalepon INDONESIA 61D
63C
Kalevala RUSSIA 29C
31B
Kaliningrad RUSSIA 31C
32A
35A
Kalinin RUSSIA 31D
32B
35B
Kaluga RUSSIA 31D
32B
35B
Kama, River RUSSIA 33A
Kamchatka Pen. SIBERIA
49D
50C
Kamensk-Ural'skij SIBERIA
33A
Kamenskoje SIBERIA 49B
Kamina ZAIRE 40D
42B
Kamloops CANADA 7C
Kampala UGANDA 41A
Kampuchea 57A
Kamysin RUSSIA 32D
35B
Kananga ZAIRE 40D
42B
Kanazawa JAPAN 55A
Kandi BENIN 36D
Kandy SRI LANKA 56C
Kangaroo I. AUSTRALIA
64D
Kanggye NORTH KOREA
55C
Kankan GUINEA 24B
36C
Kano NIGERIA 37C
Kanpur INDIA 56A
Kansas City U.S.A. 8C
11A
Kansas U.S.A. 8C
11A
Kansk SIBERIA 52B
Kansu CHINA 53C
Kaohsiung TAIWAN 57B
Kaolack SENEGAL 24A
36C
Kap Brewster
GREENLAND 21A
30A
Kap Farvel GREENLAND
21D
Kap Morris Jesup
GREENLAND 20A
Kap York GREENLAND 5D
Kapingamarangi At. 62D
Kara Sea 46A
74B
Kara TOGO 36D
Karachi PAKISTAN 39B
Karaganda KAZAKHSTAN
33D
52C
Karaginskij Zaliv 49D
50C
Karaginskij, O. SIBERIA
49D
50C
Karamay CHINA 52D
Kargasok SIBERIA 52A
Kargopol' RUSSIA 32B
Karlskrona SWEDEN 31C
Karnataka INDIA 56C
Karskje Vorota, Pr. 29D
Kasai, River ZAIRE 40D
Kasama ZAMBIA 42B
Kashi CHINA 52C
Kashmir 56A
Kassala SUDAN 38D
41A
Kathmandu NEPAL 56B
Katowice POLAND 31C
32C
35A
Kauai Hawaii (U.S.A.) 69A
Kaunas LITHUANIA 31D
32A
35A
Kayes MALI 24A
36C
Kayseri TURKEY 35D
38A
Kazakhstan 33D
Kazan Retto JAPAN 55B
Kazan RUSSIA 33A
74B
Keetmanshoop NAMIBIA
S.A. 27B
42C
Kelowna CANADA 7C
10A
Kem' RUSSIA 31B
Kemerovo SIBERIA 52A
Kendawangan INDONESIA
60D
Kenora CANADA 8C
11A
Kentucky U.S.A. 11C
Kenya 41A
Kenya, Mt. KENYA 41A
Kerc CRIMEA 32D
35B
Kerguelen Iles (FRANCE)
45B
Kermadec Is. (N.Z.) 71C
Kermadec Trench 71C
Kerman IRAN 39A
Ketchikan Alaska, U.S.A. 7A
Key West U.S.A. 11D
12B
Kharagpur INDIA 56D
Khartoum SUDAN 38C
41A
Khulna BANGLADESH 56D
Kiangsi CHINA 55D
57B
Kiangsu CHINA 55C
57B
Kiel GERMANY 31C
34B
Kiev UKRAINE 31D
32C
35A
Kiffa MAURITANIA 24A
36C
Kigali RWANDA 41C
42B
Kigoma TANZANIA 42B
Kiklades GREECE 35C
37B
38A
Kikwit ZAIRE 40D
Kilimanjaro, Mt. TANZANIA
43A
41C
Kimberley S.A. 42D
Kimch'aek NORTH KOREA
55C
Kindu ZAIRE 40D

42B
King George I. ANTARCTICA 18D
King I. AUSTRALIA 66D
King William I. CANADA 4D
Kingman Reef (U.S.A.) 69D
Kingoonya AUSTRALIA 64D
Kingston CANADA 8D 11B
Kingston JAMAICA 13A
Kingston NORFOLK ISLAND (AUSTRALIA) 66A
Kingstown ST. VINCENT AND THE GRENADINES 13D
Kinshasa ZAIRE 40C 42A
Kirensk SIBERIA 53A
Kirghizia 33D 52C
Kiribati 70C
Kiritimati I. 70A
Kirkenes NORWAY 29C 31B
Kirkuk IRAQ 38B
Kirov RUSSIA 32B
Kirovsk RUSSIA 29C 31B
Kiruna SWEDEN 28D 31A
Kisangani ZAIRE 40B
Kisin'ov MOLDAVIA 31D 32C 35A
Kisumu KENYA 41A
Kita-kyusyu JAPAN 55C
Kitale KENYA 41A
Kitwe ZAMBIA 42B
Klaipeda LITHUANIA 31C 32A 35A
Klamath Falls U.S.A. 10A
Knoxville U.S.A. 11D
Knud Rasmussen Land GREENLAND 20C
Kobe JAPAN 55A
Kodiak Alaska, U.S.A. 6A
Kodiak I. Alaska, U.S.A. 6A
Kokand 33D 52C
Kolgujev, O. RUSSIA 29D
Kolomna RUSSIA 32B 35B
Kolonia 62B
Kolpasevo SIBERIA 52A
Kolskij Poluostrov RUSSIA 29C 31B
Kolumadulu At. 58C
Kolwezi ZAIRE 40D 42B
Kolyma, River SIBERIA 48B 49A
Kolymskaja Nizmennost' SIBERIA 48B
Kolymskoje Nagorje SIBERIA 49C
Komandorskije O-va SIBERIA 50D
Komsa SIBERIA 52A
Komsomol'sk-na-Amure SIBERIA 54C
Kong Christian X Land GREENLAND 21A
Kong Frederik VI Kyst GREENLAND 21D
Kong Frederik VIII Land GREENLAND 20B
Kong Karls Land NORWAY 28B
Kor'akskoje Nagorje SIBERIA 49D
Korat THAILAND 57C
Korhogo IVORY COAST 24B 36D
Korla CHINA 52D
Kosciusko, Mt. AUSTRALIA 65C 66C
Kosice CZECHOSLOVAKIA 35A
Kostroma RUSSIA 32B 35B
Kota Bharu MALAYSIA 57C 60A
Kota Kinabalu MALAYSIA 57D
Kotel'nyj, O. SIBERIA 47B
Kotka FINLAND 31B 32A
Kotuj, River SIBERIA 47C
Kotzebue Alaska, U.S.A. 2B 74C
Kotzebue Sd. 2A
Kourou GUYANE 15A
Köln GERMANY 31C 34B
Kraków POLAND 31C 32C 35A
Krasnodar RUSSIA 32D
Krasnojarsk SIBERIA 52B
Krasnovisersk RUSSIA 33A
Krasnovodsk TURKMEN REP. 33C
Kristiansand NORWAY 31C 34B
Kristiansund NORWAY 31A
Kriti GREECE 35C 37B
Krivoj Rog UKRAINE 31D 35B
Kroonstad S.A. 42D
Kuala Lumpur MALAYSIA 60A
Kuantan MALAYSIA 60B
Kuching MALAYSIA 60D
Kudymkar RUSSIA 33A
Kujbysev RUSSIA 33A
Kujbysev SIBERIA 52A
Kumamoto JAPAN 55C
Kumasi GHANA 36D
Kunasir, O. SIBERIA 54B
Kunlun Shan CHINA 56A
Kunming CHINA 57A
Kuopio FINLAND 31B 32A
Kupang INDONESIA 61C
Kuqa CHINA 52D
Kure I. 68D
Kurgan SIBERIA 33B
Kuril Islands SIBERIA 54B
Kuril Trench 51C 54B
Kursk RUSSIA 32D 35B
Kusaie 62B
Kusiro JAPAN 54B
Kuskokwim, River Alaska, U.S.A. 2C 6A
Kustanaj KAZAKHSTAN 33B
Kutaisi GEORGIA 32D 35D
Kuujjuaq CANADA 9A
Kuusamo FINLAND 29C 31B
Kuwait 38B
Kuwait, KUWAIT 38B
Kuzomen' RUSSIA 31B
Kvitøya NORWAY 28B
Kwajalein At. 62A
Kwangju SOUTH KOREA 55C
Kwangsi Chuang CHINA 57A
Kwangtung CHINA 55D 57B
Kweichow CHINA 57A
Kyoto JAPAN 55A
Kyra SIBERIA 53A
Kyzyl SIBERIA 52B
Kzyl-Orda KAZAKHSTAN 33D

L

L'achovskije O-va SIBERIA 48A
l'Est, I. de (FRANCE) 45A
L'vov UKRAINE 31D 32C 35A
La Ceiba HONDURAS 12D
La Coruña SPAIN 23B 34C
La Crosse U.S.A. 8C 11A
La Loche CANADA 7D 8A
La Palma Canary Islands (SPAIN) 23C 36A
La Palma PANAMA 14A
La Paloma URAGUAY 17C
La Pampa ARGENTINA 16D
La Paz BOLIVIA 14D 16B
La Paz MEXICO 10C 12C
La Pérouse Strait 54B
La Plata ARGENTINA 16D
La Qiuaca ARGENTINA 14D 16B
La Rioja ARGENTINA 16B
La Serena CHILE 16A
Laâyoune MOROCCO 23D 36A
Labé GUINEA 24B 36C
Labrador CANADA 9A
Labrador City CANADA 9C
Labrador Sea 9B
Labytnangi SIBERIA 46C
Laccadive Is. (INDIA) 39D 56C
Laccadive Sea 39D 56C
Ladakh Kashmir INDIA 56A
Ladozskoje Ozero 31B 32A
Ladysmith S.A. 42D
Laghouat ALGERIA 36B
Lagos NIGERIA 36D 40A
Lahore PAKISTAN 39B 56A
Laiagam P.N.G. 63C
Lajes BRAZIL 17A
Lambaréné GABON 40A
Lambasa FIJI 70D
Lamotrek At. 62D
Lanai Hawaii (U.S.A.) 69A
Lancaster Sound 5C
Lansing U.S.A. 8D 11B
Lanzarote Canary Islands (SPAIN) 23D 36A
Lanzhou CHINA 57A
Lao Cai VIETNAM 57C
Laoag PHILIPPINES 57D
Laos 57C 60A
Lapland FINLAND 28D 31B
Laptev Sea 47A 74A
Las Cruces U.S.A. 10D
Las Palmas Canary Islands (SPAIN) 23C 36A
Las Vegas U.S.A. 10C
Latvia 31D 32A 35A
Lau Group 70D
Launceston Tasmania, AUSTRALIA 66D
Lavongai P.N.G. 62D
Laysan I. Hawaii (U.S.A.) 69C
Lárissa GREECE 32C 35C
Le Havre FRANCE 30D 34A
Le Mans FRANCE 30D 34A
Lebanon 35D 38A
Leeds U.K. 30D 34A
Leeuwin, C. AUSTRALIA 64C
Legaspi PHILIPPINES 61A
Leh Kashmir, INDIA 56A
Leipzig GERMANY 31C 34B
Lena, River SIBERIA 47D 48A
Leninakan ARMENIA 32D
Leningrad RUSSIA 31B
Lenkoran AZERBAIJAN 33C 38B
Lensk SIBERIA 47D 74A
León MEXICO 12A
León NICARAGUA 12D
Leshan CHINA 57A
Lesotho 42D
Lesser Antilles 13C
Lethbridge CANADA 7D 10B
Lhasa CHINA 56B
Lianyungang CHINA 55C 57B
Liaoning CHINA 55C

Liaoyuan CHINA 54D
Liberia 24B 36C
Libreville GABON 40A
Libya 37A
Libyan Desert see As Sahra al Libiyah
Liechenstein 31C 34B
Lifou 63B
Likasi ZAIRE 40D 42B
Lille FRANCE 30D 34B
Lilongwe MALAWI 41C 43A
Lima PERU 14C
Limoges FRANCE 34A
Lincoln Sea 20C
Lincoln U.S.A. 8C 11A
Lindi TANZANIA 41C 43A
Line Islands 69B 70A
Lingga, Kep. INDONESIA 60D
Linhe CHINA 53C
Linxia CHINA 57A
Lipeck RUSSIA 32B 35B
Lisala ZAIRE 37D 40B
Lisbon PORTUGAL 23D 34C
Lisianski I. Hawaii (U.S.A.) 69C
Lithuania 31D 32A 35A
Little Rock U.S.A. 11C
Liuzhou CHINA 57A
Liverpool U.K. 23B 30D 34A
Livingstone ZAMBIA 40D 42B
Ljubljana YUGOSLAVIA 34B
Lobito ANGOLA 40C 42A
Lodejnoje Pole RUSSIA 31B 32A
Lodwar KENYA 41A
Lofoten NORWAY 28D 31A
Logan, Mt. CANADA 2D 6B
Loire, River FRANCE 30D 34B
Loma Mts SIERRA LEONE 36C
Lomé TOGO 36D
London CANADA 8D 11B
London U.K. 23B 30D 34A
Londonderry U.K. 30D 34A
Londrina BRAZIL 15C 17A
Long I. BAHAMAS 11D 13A
Longyearbyen (NORWAY) 28B
Lop Nur CHINA 52D
Lopatka, M. SIBERIA 50D 54A
Lord Howe Is. (AUSTRALIA) 65D 66C
Los Angeles U.S.A. 10C
Los Mochis MEXICO 10D
Louangphrabang LAOS 57C 60A
Loubomo CONGO 40C 42A
Lougheed I. CANADA 4B
Louisbourg CANADA 9D
Louisiade Arch. 63C
Louisiana U.S.A. 11C 12B
Louisville U.S.A. 11D
Lódz POLAND 31C 35A
Luanda ANGOLA 40C 42A
Lubbock U.S.A. 10D
Lübeck GERMANY 31C 34B
Lublin POLAND 32C 35A
Lubumbashi ZAIRE 40D 42B
Lüderitz NAMIBIA S.A. 42C 27B
Ludhiana INDIA 39B 56A
Luena ANGOLA 40D
Luleå SWEDEN 31A 74B
Luoyang CHINA 57B
Lupanshui CHINA 57A
Lusaka ZAMBIA 40D 42B
Luxembourg 30D 34B
Luxor EGYPT 38A
Luzon I. PHILIPPINES 61A
Luzon Strait 57D
Lynn Lake CANADA 8A
Lyon FRANCE 34B

M

M'Clintock Channel 4D
M'Clure Strait 4A
McKean I. 70C
McKinley, Mt. Alaska, U.S.A. 2D
McMurdo (U.S.A.) ANTARCTICA 75B
MacRobertson Coast ANTARCTICA 45C
Macapá BRAZIL 15A
Macau (PORTUGAL) 55D 57D
Macaulay I. 71C
Macdonnell Ras. AUSTRALIA 64B
Maceió BRAZIL 15D 25C
Machackala RUSSIA 33C
Machu Picchu PERU 14C
Mackay AUSTRALIA 63D 65B
Mackenzie King I. CANADA 4B
Mackenzie Mountains CANADA 3C 7A
Mackenzie, River CANADA 3D 74C
Maclean Strait 4B
Macon U.S.A. 11D
Macquarie I. (AUSTRALIA) 67D
Madagascar 41D 43B
Madang P.N.G. 63C
Madeira Islands (PORTUGAL) 23C 36A
Madeira, River BRAZIL 14D
Madison U.S.A. 11A
Madras INDIA 56C
Madrid SPAIN 23B 34C
Madura INDONESIA 60D
Madurai INDIA 56C
Mafia I. TANZANIA 41C 43A
Magadan SIBERIA 49C
Magallanes, Estr. de 18A
Magdalena, River COLOMBIA 13C 14A
Magellan Str. of see Magallanes, Estr. de
Magnitogorsk RUSSIA 33A
Mahajanga MADAGASCAR 41D 43B
Maharashtra INDIA 56C
Mahé I. SEYCHELLES 41D 43B 58D
Maiduguri NIGERIA 37C
Maine U.S.A. 9C
Majene INDONESIA 61C
Majuro At. 62B
Makemo 70B 72A
Makurdi NIGERIA 37C 40A
Mal. Tajmyr, O. SIBERIA 46B
Malaita SOLOMON ISLANDS 63A
Malakal SUDAN 37D 38C 41A
Malang INDONESIA 60D
Malawi 41C 43A
Malawi, L. MALAWI 41C 43A
Malaysia 60B
Maldives 58A
Mali 24A 36D
Malmberget SWEDEN 28D 31A
Malmesbury S.A. 27D 42C
Malmö SWEDEN 31C
Maloelap Atoll 62B
Malosmadulu At. 58C
Malpelo I. de (COLOMBIA) 12D
Malta 34D 37A
Mamonuito Atoll 62D
Mamou GUINEA 24B 36C
Manado INDONESIA 61C
Managua NICARAGUA 12D
Manama BAHRAIN 39A
Mananjary MADAGASCAR 43D
Manaus BRAZIL 14B
Manchester U.K. 23B 30D 34A
Manchuria CHINA 54D
Mandalay BURMA 57C
Mangaia 71A
Mangalore INDIA 39D 56C
Mangareva 72C
Manicouagan Resérvoir CANADA 9C
Maniitsoq (Sukkertoppen) GREENLAND 21C
Manila PHILIPPINES 57D 61A
Manitoba CANADA 8A
Manizales COLOMBIA 14A
Mansel I. CANADA 9A
Manua Is. 70D
Manus 62D
Manzanillo MEXICO 12A
Manzhouli CHINA 53B
Maputo MOZAMBIQUE 43C
Mar del Plata ARGENTINA 17C
Maracaibo VENEZUELA 13C 14A
Maracaibo, L. de VENEZUELA 13C 14A
Marambio (ARGENTINA) ANTARCTICA 19C 75C
Maranhão BRAZIL 15A
Marañón, River PERU 14A
Maré 63B
Margarita, I. VENEZUELA 13D 14B
Maria 71A
Marian I.(S.A.) 44B
Mariana Islands 62C
Mariana Trench 62C
Marie Byrd Land ANTARCTICA 75D
Maringá BRAZIL 15C 17A
Mariscal Estigarribia PARAGUAY 14D 16B
Mariupol UKRAINE 32D 35B
Markovo SIBERIA 49B
Marquesas Is. see Marquises, Iles
Marquises, Iles 72A
Marrakech MOROCCO 23D 34C 36A
Marsabit KENYA 41A
Marseille FRANCE 34D
Marshall Islands 62A
Marutea 72C
Maryborough AUSTRALIA 63D 65B

Maryland U.S.A. 11D
Masbate PHILIPPINES 61A
Mascarene Islands 43D 59C
Maseru LESOTHO 42D
Mashhad IRAN 39A
Mata'utu WALLIS IS. (FRANCE) 70D
Matadi ZAIRE 40C 42A
Matagami CANADA 9C 11B
Matamoros MEXICO 10D 12A
Mato Grosso BRAZIL 15C 17A
Maug Is. 62C
Maui Hawaii (U.S.A.) 69A
Mauke 70B
Maupiti Iles de la Société 70B
Mauritania 24A 36C
Mauritius 59C
Mawson (AUSTRALIA) ANTARCTICA 45C 75A
Mayo CANADA 3C 7A
Mayotte (FRANCE) 41D
Mazar-e Sharif AFGHANISTAN 39B
Mazatlán MEXICO 10D 12A
Mbabane SWAZILAND 42D
Mbala ZAMBIA 42B
Mbandaka ZAIRE 40B
Mbeya TANZANIA 41C 43A
Mbuji-Mayi ZAIRE 40D 42B
Mecca SAUDI ARABIA 38D
Medan INDONESIA 60A
Medellín COLOMBIA 13C 14A
Medicine Hat CANADA 7D 10B
Medina SAUDI ARABIA 38B
Mediterranean Sea 34D 35C
Mednyj, O. SIBERIA 50D
Medvezjegorsk RUSSIA 31B 32A
Medvezji O-va SIBERIA 48B
Meerut INDIA 56A
Meighen I. CANADA 5A
Meiktila BURMA 57C 60A
Meknès MOROCCO 23D 36B
Mekong, River 57C
Melanesia 62B 63A
Melbourne AUSTRALIA 65C 66D
Melilla (SPAIN) 34C 36B
Melitopol UKRAINE 32D 35B
Melville Bugt GREENLAND 5D 20D
Melville I. AUSTRALIA 61D 64B
Melville I. CANADA 4B
Melville Pen. CANADA 5C
Memphis U.S.A. 11C
Mendoza ARGENTINA 16D
Menongue ANGOLA 40D 42A
Menorca SPAIN 34D
Merauke INDONESIA 61D
Mercy, C CANADA 9B
Mergui BURMA 57C 60A
Messina Sicilia, ITALY 34D
Messina S.A. 42D
Mexico 12A
Mexico MEXICO 12A
Mezen' RUSSIA 29D
Mérida MEXICO 12B
Mérida VENEZUELA 13C 14A
Miami U.S.A. 11D
Michigan U.S.A. 8D 11B
Michigan, L. U.S.A. 8D 11B
Michikamau, L. CANADA 9B
Midway Is. (U.S.A.) 68D
Mil'kovo SIBERIA 49D 50D 54A
Miladummadulu Atoll MALDIVES 56C 58A
Milano ITALY 34B
Mildura AUSTRALIA 65C 66C
Mili At. 62B
Milwaukee U.S.A. 8D 11A
Mimika INDONESIA 61D
Minas Gerais BRAZIL 15C 17A
Mindanao I. PHILIPPINES 61A
Mindoro I. PHILIPPINES 57D 61A
Minneapolis U.S.A. 8C 11A
Minnesota U.S.A. 8C 11A
Minot U.S.A. 7D 8C 11A
Minsk BYELORUSSIA 31D 32A 35A
Miracema do Tocantins BRAZIL 15C
Mirnyj SIBERIA 47D
Misiones ARGENTINA 17A
Miskolc HUNGARY 31C 32C 35A
Misrātah LIBYA 34D 37A
Mississippi U.S.A. 11C
Mississippi, River U.S.A. 8C 11A 11C
Missouri U.S.A. 11C
Missouri, River U.S.A 7D 8C 10B 11A
Mistassini, L. CANADA 9C
Mitsiwa ETHIOPIA 38D
Mo i Rana NORWAY 28D 31A
Mobile U.S.A. 11C 12B
Moçambique MOZAMBIQUE 41C 43A
Moe AUSTRALIA 65C 66D
Mogadishu SOMALIA 41B
Mogil'ov BYELORUSSIA 31D 32A 35A
Mogoca SIBERIA 53B
Moldavia 31D 32C 35A
Molod'oznaja ANTARCTICA 44D 75A
Molokai Hawaii (U.S.A.) 69A
Moluccas INDONESIA 61C
Mombasa KENYA 41C 43A
Monaco 34D
Moncton CANADA 9C
Mongolia 53C
Mongu ZAMBIA 40D 42B
Monrovia LIBERIA 24B 36C
Mont Forel GREENLAND 21C
Montague I. 19B
Montague I. Alaska, U.S.A. 2D 6B
Montana U.S.A. 7D 10B
Montego Bay JAMAICA 13A
Monterey U.S.A. 10C
Monteria COLOMBIA 13C 14A
Monterrey MEXICO 10D 12A
Montes Claros BRAZIL 15C 17A
Montevideo URAGUAY 17C
Montgomery U.S.A. 11C 12B
Montpelier U.S.A. 9C
Montpellier FRANCE 34D
Montréal CANADA 9C
Montserrat (U.K.) 13D
Moose Jaw CANADA 7D 10B
Moosonee CANADA 8D 11B
Mora SWEDEN 31A
Morioka JAPAN 55A
Morocco 23D 34C 36B
Morondava MADAGASCAR 43C
Moroni COMOROS 41D
Morotai INDONESIA 61D
Moscow RUSSIA 32B 35B
Mossel Bay S.A. 42D
Mossoro BRAZIL 15B 25C
Mosul IRAQ 38B
Motu One Iles de la Société 70B
Moulmein BURMA 57C 60A
Mount Gambier AUSTRALIA 65C
Mount Isa AUSTRALIA 63D 65A
Moyale KENYA 41A
Mozambique 43A
Mozambique Channel 41C 43A
Mt. Ross Kerguelen Iles (FRANCE) 45B
Mt. Blanc FRANCE 34B
Mtito Andei KENYA 41C 43A
Mudanjiang CHINA 54D
Mui Bai Bung VIETNAM 57C 60B
Mujnak UZBEKISTAN 33C
Multan PAKISTAN 39B 56A
Murmansk RUSSIA 29C 31B 74B
Murray, River AUSTRALIA 65C
Mururoa 72C
Muscat OMAN 39A
Mutare ZIMBABWE 41C 43A
München GERMANY 31C 34B
Mwanza TANZANIA 41C 43A
Mys Cel'uskin SIBERIA 46B
Mysore INDIA 56C

N

N'dalatando ANGOLA 40C 42A
N'Djamena CHAD 37C 40A
N'urba SIBERIA 47D
Nachicevan ARMENIA 38B
Nachodka SIBERIA 54D
Nadym SIBERIA 46C
Nagasaki JAPAN 55C
Nagoya JAPAN 55A
Nagpur INDIA 56C
Naha JAPAN 55D
Nain CANADA 9B
Nairobi KENYA 41C 43A
Naknek Alaska, U.S.A. 2C 6A
Nal'cik RUSSIA 32D
Namangan 33D 52C
Namcy SIBERIA 48C
Namibe ANGOLA 26B 40C 42A
Namibia S.A. 27B 42C
Nampula MOZAMBIQUE 41C 43A
Nanchang CHINA 55D 57B
Nancy FRANCE 30D 34B
Nanking CHINA 55D

57B
Nanortalik GREENLAND 21D
Nanping CHINA 55D
Nanpo Syoto 55B
Nantes FRANCE 23B 30D 34A
Nanyuki KENYA 41A
Napo, River PERU 14A
Napoli ITALY 34D
Nares Strait 20C
Narjan-Mar 29D 74B
Narsarsuaq GREENLAND 21D
Narvik NORWAY 28D 31A
Nashik INDIA 39D 56C
Nashville U.S.A. 11C
Nassau BAHAMAS 11D 13A
Nassau Cook Islands 70D
Natal BRAZIL 15D 25C
Natchez U.S.A. 11C 12B
Natuna P. MALAYSIA 60B
Nauru 62B
Nazca PERU 14C 16A
Ndélé C.A.R. 37D 40B
Ndola ZAIRE 40D
Ndzouani COMOROS 41D
Near Islands ALASKA 50D
Nebraska U.S.A. 8C 11A
Necker I. Hawaii (U.S.A.) 69C
Necochea ARGENTINA 17C
Ned. Antillen (NETHERLANDS) 13B
Negros I. PHILIPPINES 61A
Neijiang CHINA 57A
Nellore INDIA 56C
Nelson, River CANADA 8A
Nelva COLOMBIA 13C
Nemuro JAPAN 54B
Nenjiang CHINA 54D
Nepal 56B
Netherlands, The 30D 34B
Neuquén ARGENTINA 16D
Nevada U.S.A. 10A
New Amsterdam GUYANA 14B
New Britain P.N.G. 63C
New Brunswick CANADA 9C
New Caledonia see Nouvelle Calédonie
New Delhi INDIA 56A
New Guinea 63C
New Hampshire U.S.A. 9C
New Haven U.S.A. 9C
New Ireland P.N.G. 63C
New Jersey U.S.A. 9C
New Mexico U.S.A. 10D
New Orleans U.S.A. 11C 12B
New Plymouth N.Z. 66B
New Siberian Islands SIBERIA 47B
74A
New South Wales AUSTRALIA 65C 66C
New York State U.S.A. 8D 11B
New York U.S.A. 9C 11B
New Zealand 66B
Newark U.S.A. 9C 11B
Newcastle AUSTRALIA 65D 66C
Newcastle U.K. 30D 34A
Newfoundland CANADA 9B 22A
Newfoundland, Island of CANADA 9D 22A
Newport News U.S.A. 11D
Néma MAURITANIA 24A 36C
Ngaoundére CAMEROON 37C 40A
Ngazidja COMOROS 41C 43A
Nguigmi NIGER 37C 40A
Nha Trang VIETNAM 57C 60B
Niagara Falls CANADA 8D 11B
Niagara Falls U.S.A. 8D 11B
Niamey NIGER 36D
Nicaragua 12D
Nicaragua, L. de NICARAGUA 12D
Nice FRANCE 34D
Nicobar Is. (INDIA) 60A
Nicosia CYPRUS 35D 37B 38A
Niger 37C 40A
Niger, River MALI 24A 36D
Niger, River NIGERIA 36D 40A
Nigeria 37C 40A
Nihoa Hawaii (U.S.A.) 69A
Niigata JAPAN 55A
Nikolajevsk-na-Amure SIBERIA 54C
Nikumaroro 70C
Nile, River EGYPT 37B 38A
Ningbo CHINA 55D 57B
Ningsia Hui CHINA 53C
Nipigon CANADA 8D 11B
Nipigon, L. CANADA 8D 11B
Niterói BRAZIL 15D 17B
Niue I. (N.Z.) 70D
Niznevartovsk SIBERIA 33B 52A
Niznij Novgorod RUSSIA 32B 35B
Niznij Tagil SIBERIA 33A
Nizwa OMAN 39C
Nogales MEXICO 10D
Nome Alaska, U.S.A. 2C
Nomoi Is. 62D
Nomuka Group 70D
Nordaustlandet NORWAY 28B
Nordensel'da, Arch SIBERIA 46B
Nordvik SIBERIA 47A
Norfolk Island (AUSTRALIA) 66A
Norfolk U.S.A. 11D
Noril'sk SIBERIA 46D 74B
Norrköping SWEDEN 31C 34B
Norske Øer GREENLAND 20B
North Atlantic Ocean 22B 23D 68A
North Battleford CANADA 7D
North Bay CANADA 8D 11B
North Cape N.Z. 66A
North Cape NORWAY 28D 74B
North Carolina U.S.A. 11D
North Dakota U.S.A. 7D 8C 11A
North Island N.Z. 66B 71D
North Korea 55C
North Land SIBERIA 46A 74A
North Magnetic Pole 5A 74D
North Pacific Ocean 51B
North Platte U.S.A. 8C 10B
North Pole 75A
North Sea 34A 34B
North West Cape AUSTRALIA 64A
North West Territories CANADA 4C 7B
Northam AUSTRALIA 64C
Northern Mariana Islands 62C
Northern Territory AUSTRALIA 64B
Norton Sound 2C
Norway 28D 31A 74B
Norwegian Sea 28C 30B 74B
Norwich U.K. 30D 34A
Nottingham I. CANADA 9A
Nouâdhibou MAURITANIA 24A 36C
Nouakchott MAURITANIA 24A 36C
Nouméa 63B
Nouvelle-Calédonie (FRANCE) 63B
Nova Iguacu BRAZIL 17A 15C
Nova Scotia CANADA 9C
Novaja Zeml'a 29D 74B
Novgorod RUSSIA 31D 32A
Novokuzneck SIBERIA 52B
Novosibirsk SIBERIA 52A
Novyj Port SIBERIA 46C
Nuevo Laredo MEXICO 10D 12A
Nuku Hiva 72A
Nuku'alofa TONGA 71C
Nukunono 70C
Nukuoro At. 62D
Nukus UZBEKISTAN 33C
Nullarbor Plain AUSTRALIA 64D
Nunivak I. Alaska, U.S.A. 2C 6A
Nuuk (Godthåb) GREENLAND 21D 74D
Nürnberg GERMANY 31C 34B
Nzérékore GUINEA 24B 36C

O

Oakland U.S.A. 10A
Oauhu Hawaii (U.S.A.) 69A
Oaxaca MEXICO 12A
Ob', River SIBERIA 33B 52A
Oblucie SIBERIA 54D
Obskaja Guba 46C
Ocha SIBERIA 54C
Ochotsk SIBERIA 48D
Odense DENMARK 31C 34B
Oder, River GERMANY 31C
Oder, River POLAND 34B
Odessa UKRAINE 31D 32C 35A
Odessa U.S.A 12A 10D
Oeno I. 72D
Ogden U.S.A. 10B
Ohio U.S.A. 8D 11B
Ohio, River U.S.A. 8D 11A
Ojm'akon SIBERIA 48D
Oka, River RUSSIA 35B
Okhotsk, Sea of 49C 54A
Okinawa JAPAN 55D
Oklahoma City U.S.A. 11C
Oklahoma U.S.A. 11C
Ol'utorskij SIBERIA 50C
Ol'utorskij, M. SIBERIA 49D
Ol'utorskij Zaliv 49D
Ola SIBERIA 49C
Oland SWEDEN 31C
Olavarría ARGENTINA 16D
Olen'ok SIBERIA 47D
Olen'ok, River SIBERIA 47B
Olen'okskij Zaliv 47B
Olympia U.S.A. 7C 10A
Olympus GREECE 32C 35C

Omaha U.S.A. 8C 11A
Oman 39C
Omdurman SUDAN 37D 38C 41A
Omsk SIBERIA 33B 52A
Omsukcan SIBERIA 49C
Onezskoje Oz. RUSSIA 31B 32A
Onslow AUSTRALIA 64A
Ontario CANADA 8D 11B
Ontario, L. CANADA 8D 11B
Ontario, L. U.S.A. 8D 11B
Or'ol RUSSIA 32B 35B
Oran ALGERIA 34C 36B
Orange AUSTRALIA 65C 66C
Orange River S.A. 42C
Orange, River Namibia, S.A. 27B
Orcadas (ARGENTINA) ANTARCTICA 19C 75C
Orebro SWEDEN 31C
Orechovo-Zujevo RUSSIA 32B 35B
Oregon U.S.A. 10A
Orenburg RUSSIA 33A
Orinoco, River VENEZUELA 13D 14B
Orissa INDIA 56D
Orizaba MEXICO 12A
Orkney Is. (U.K.) 30D
Orlando U.S.A. 11D 13A
Orsk RUSSIA 33C
Orumiyeh IRAN 32D 38B
Oruro BOLIVIA 14D 16B
Osaka JAPAN 55A
Oshogbo NIGERIA 36D 40A
Oslo NORWAY 31C
Ostersund SWEDEN 31A
Ostrava CZECHOSLOVAKIA 31C
Ostrov Paramusir SIBERIA 50D 54A
Ostrov Sachalin SIBERIA 54A
Osumi So. JAPAN 55D
Ottawa CANADA 9C 11B
Ottawa I. CANADA 9A
Ouagadougou BURKINA FASO 36D
Ouahigouya BURKINA FASO 24B
Ouargla ALGERIA 36B
Ouarzazate MOROCCO 34C 36B
Oudskoje Ozera Estonia 31D 32A 35A
Oudtshoorn S.A. 42D
Ouesso CONGO 40A
Oujda MOROCCO 23D 34C 36B
Oulu FINLAND 74B
Ouro Preto BRAZIL 15C 17A
Ouvéa 63B
Oviedo SPAIN 23B 34C
Ozero Bajkal RUSSIA 53A
Ozero Balchas KAZAKHSTAN 52C

P

Paamiut (Frederikshåb) GREENLAND 21D
Pachaci SIBERIA 49D
Pacific Ocean 75D
Padang INDONESIA 60C
Pagan BURMA 56D 60A
Pagan MARIANA IS. 62C
Pagula (EQUATORIAL GUINEA) 40B
Pakistan 39B
Pakxé LAOS 57C
Palau 61B
Palawan PHILIPPINES 57D 61A
Palembang INDONESIA 60D
Palermo SICILY, ITALY 34D
Palliser, C. N.Z. 66B
Palliser, Iles Tuamotu Islands 72A 70B
Palma Mallorca, SPAIN 34D
Palmer (U.S.A.) ANTARCTICA 18D 75C
Palmerston North N.Z. 66B
Palmyra I. (U.S.A.) 69D
Paloh INDONESIA 60D
Pamir TADZHIKISTAN 39B 56A
Panaji INDIA 39D 56C
Panama 12D 14A
Panama Canal 13C 14A
Panama PANAMA 13C 14A
Panay I. PHILIPPINES 61A
Pangnirtung CANADA 5D
Papua New Guinea 63C
Papua, G. of 63C
Pará BRAZIL 15C
Paracel Is. 57D 60B
Paraguay 14D 16B
Paraguay, River PARAGUAY 14D 16B
Paraiba BRAZIL 15D 25C
Paramaribo SURINAME 13D 15A
Parana BRAZIL 17A
Parana, River BRAZIL 15C 17A
Paraná ARGENTINA 16B
Paraná, River ARGENTINA 16B
Paris FRANCE 30D 34B
Parnaíba BRAZIL 15B
Parry Is. CANADA 4B 74C
Parry Sound CANADA 8D 11B
Pasni PAKISTAN 39B
Passo Fundo BRAZIL 17A
Pasto COLOMBIA 13C 14A
Patagonia ARGENTINA 18A
Patan NEPAL 56B
Patna INDIA 56B
Pátra GREECE 32C 35C
Paulo Afonso BRAZIL 15D 25C
Pavlodar KAZAKHSTAN 33B 52A
Paysandu URAGUAY 16B
Pärnu ESTONIA 31D 32A 35A
Peace, River CANADA 7B
Peary Channel 5A
Pecora RUSSIA 29D
Pecora, River RUSSIA 29D
Pecorskoje More 29D
Pegu BURMA 60A
Pehuajó ARGENTINA 16D
Peking CHINA 53D 55C
Pemba I. TANZANIA 41C 43A
Pemba MOZAMBIQUE 43A
Penedos de S. Pedro e S. Paulo (BRAZIL) 24D
Pennsylvania U.S.A. 8D 11B
Penrhyn At. 70A
Pensacola U.S.A. 11C 12B
Penza RUSSIA 32B 35B
Penzinskaja Guba 49D
Peoria U.S.A. 8C 11A
Perito Moreno ARGENTINA 16D 18A
Perm' RUSSIA 33A
Pernambuco BRAZIL 15D
Perpignan FRANCE 34D
Perth AUSTRALIA 64C
Peru 14C
Peru-Chile Trench 14C 16A
Pescara ITALY 34D
Peshawar PAKISTAN 39B 56A
Petra, O. va SIBERIA 47A
Petropavlovsk KAZAKHSTAN 33B
Petropovlovsk-Kamcatskij SIBERIA 50D
Petrozavodsk RUSSIA 31B 32A
Pevek SIBERIA 49A
Pécs HUNGARY 35A
Philadelphia U.S.A. 8D 11B
Philippine Sea 61B
Philippine Trench 61A 61B
Philippines 61A
Phitsanulok THAILAND 57C 60A
Phoenix Islands 70C
Phoenix U.S.A 10C
Phuket THAILAND 60A
Piauí BRAZIL 15C
Pickle Lake CANADA 8D 11A
Pico, I. (PORTUGAL) 22D
Picos BRAZIL 15D
Picton N.Z. 66B
Pierre U.S.A. 8C 11A
Pietermaritzburg S.A. 42D
Pietersburg S.A. 42D
Pik Kommunizma TADZHIKISTAN 33D 52C
Pik Pobedy KIRGHIZIA 52C
Pilcomayo, River ARGENTINA 16B
Pinamar ARGENTINA 17C
Pingelap 62B
Pingouins, I. des (FRANCE) 45A
Pinos, I. de CUBA 12B
Pins, I. des 63B
Pinsk BYELORUSSIA 31D 32C 35A
Pioner, O. SIBERIA 46A
Pirapora BRAZIL 15C 17A
Pisa ITALY 34D
Pitcairn (U.K.) 72D
Pitcairn I. 72D
Pitt I. N.Z. 67A
Pittsburgh U.S.A. 8D 11B
Piura PERU 14A
Plateau of Tibet CHINA 56A 56B
Platte, River U.S.A. 8C 11A
Plovdiv BULGARIA 32C 35C
Plymouth U.K. 23B 30D 34A
Plzen CZECHOSLOVAKIA 31C 34B
Po, River ITALY 34D
Podkamennaja Tunguska, River SIBERIA 52B
Podol'sk RUSSIA 32B 35B
Pohnpei 62B
Point Barrow Alaska, U.S.A. 2B
Pointe-à-Pitre GUADALOUPE 13B
Pointe-Noire CONGO 40C 42A
Poland 31C 32C 35A
Poltava UKRAINE 32D 35B
Poluostrov Tajmyr

SIBERIA 46B
Polynesia 70C
Pond Inlet CANADA 5C 74D
Pondicherry INDIA 56C
Ponta Delgado (PORTUGAL) 23C
Ponta Grossa BRAZIL 17A
Pontianak INDONESIA 60D
Poopó, L. BOLIVIA 14D 16B
Popayán COLOMBIA 13C 14A
Poranajsk U.S.S.R. 54A
Porbandar INDIA 39D
Porcupine, River Alaska, U.S.A. 3C
Port Augusta AUSTRALIA 65C
Port Blair Andaman Is. (INDIA) 56D 60A
Port Elizabeth S.A. 42D
Port Harcourt NIGERIA 40A
Port Hardy CANADA 7C
Port Hedland AUSTRALIA 64A
Port Lincoln AUSTRALIA 64D
Port Louis Mascarene Islands MAURITIUS 43D 59C
Port Macquarie AUSTRALIA 65D 66C
Port Moresby P.N.G. 63C
Port of Spain TRINIDAD AND TOBAGO 13D 14B
Port Pirie AUSTRALIA 65C
Port Said EGYPT 35D 37B 38A
Port Shepstone S.A. 42D
Port-au-Prince HAITI 13A
Port-aux-Français Kerguelen Iles (FRANCE) 45B
Port-Gentil GABON 40A
Portland U.S.A. 7C 10A
Portland U.S.A. 9C
Porto Alegre BRAZIL 17A
Porto Novo BENIN 36D
Porto PORTUGAL 23B 34C
Porto Velho BRAZIL 14D
Portugal 23D 34C
Posadas ARGENTINA 17A
Poste-de-la-Baleine CANADA 9A
Potosi BOLIVIA 14D 16B
Povungnituk CANADA 9A
Poznan POLAND 31C 35A
Prague CZECHOSLOVAKIA 31C 34B
Praia CAPE VERDE 24C
Praslin I. SEYCHELLES 43B 58D
Pretoria S.A. 42D
Pribilof Is. ALASKA 50A
Prince Albert CANADA 7D 8A
Prince Charles I. CANADA 5C
Prince Edward I. CANADA 9C
Prince Edward I. (S.A.) 44B
Prince George CANADA 7C
Prince Gustaf-Adolf Sea 4B
Prince of Wales I. CANADA 4D
Prince Olav Coast ANTARCTICA 44D
Prince Patrick I. CANADA 4B
Prince Rupert CANADA 7C
Princesa, Pto. PHILIPPINES 57D 61A
Proliv Longa 2A
Prome BURMA 56D 60A
Providence U.S.A. 9C
Providence, C. N.Z. 67A
Providenija SIBERIA 2C
Przeval'sk KIRGHIZIA. 52C
Pskov RUSSIA 31D 32A 35A
Pto. Cabezas NICARAGUA 12D
Pto. Limón COSTA RICA 12D
Pto. Maldonado PERU 14C
Pto. Princesa PHILIPPINES 57D 61A
Pucallpa PERU 14C
Puebla MEXICO 12A
Pueblo U.S.A 10B
Puerto Aisén CHILE 16D 18A
Puerto Baquerizo Galápagos Islands 12D
Puerto Deseado ARGENTINA 18A
Puerto Montt CHILE 16C
Puerto Natales CHILE 18A
Puerto Rico (U.S.A.) 13B
Puerto S. Julián ARGENTINA 18A
Puerto Vallerta MEXICO 12A
Pulap At. 62D
Puncak Jaya INDONESIA 61D
Pune INDIA 39D 56C
Punjab INDIA 39B 56A
Puno PERU 14C 16A
Punta Arenas CHILE 18A
Punta del Este URAGUAY 17C
Puntarenas COSTA RICA 12D
Puri INDIA 56D
Purus, River BRAZIL 14D
Pusan SOUTH KOREA 55C
Pyongyang NORTH KOREA 55C
Pyramids EGYPT 35D 37B 38A
Pyrénées FRANCE 34C

Q

Qaanaaq (Thule) GREENLAND 5B 74D
Qandahar AFGHANISTAN 39B
Qaqortoq (Julianehåb) GREENLAND 21D
Qasigiannguit (Christianshåb) GREENLAND 21C
Qatar 39A
Qeqertarsuaq (Godhavn) GREENLAND 21C
Qiemo CHINA 52D
Qigihar CHINA 53D 54D
Qingdao CHINA 55C 57B
Qinhuangdao CHINA 53D 55C
Qizan SAUDI ARABIA 38D
Quanzhou CHINA 55D 57B
Quarzazate MOROCCO 23D
Québec CANADA 9C
Queen Charlotte Islands 6D
Queen Charlotte Sound 7C
Queen Elizabeth Is. CANADA 74C 4B
Queen Mary Coast ANTARCTICA 75B
Queen Maud G. 4D
Queen Maud Land ANTARCTICA 44C 75A
Queensland AUSTRALIA 63D 65A
Queenstown S.A. 42D
Quelimane MOZAMBIQUE 41C
Querétaro MEXICO 12A
Quetta PAKISTAN 39B
Quezaltenango GUATEMALA 12D
Quezon City PHILIPPINES 57D 61A
Qui Nhon VIETNAM 57C 60B
Quito ECUADOR 14A
Quixadá BRAZIL 15B

R

R'azan RUSSIA 32B 35B
Rabat MOROCCO 23D 34C
Radisson CANADA 9A
Rainier, Mt. U.S.A. 7C 10A
Raipur INDIA 56C
Raivavae 71A 72C
Rajasthan INDIA 39B 56A
Rajkot INDIA 39D
Raleigh U.S.A. 11D
Rangiroa Tuamoto Islands 70B
Rangoon see Yangon
Rantepao INDONESIA 61C
Raoul I. 71C
Rapa 72C
Rapid City U.S.A. 8C 10B
Rasht IRAN 33C 38B
Rat Islands Alaska, U.S.A. 50B
Rawalpindi PAKISTAN 39B 56A
Rawson ARGENTINA 16D
Recherche, Arch. of the AUSTRALIA 64C
Recife BRAZIL 15D 25C
Red Sea 38D
Redding U.S.A. 10A
Reganne ALGERIA 36B
Regensburg GERMANY 31C
Regina CANADA 7D 8C 10B
Reina Adelaida, Arch. CHILE 18A
Reindeer Lake CANADA 8A
Rennell I. SOLOMON ISLANDS 63A
Rennes FRANCE 23B 30D 34A
Reno U.S.A. 10A
Resistencia ARGENTINA 16B
Resolute CANADA 5A 75A
Resolution I. CANADA 9B
Revelstoke CANADA 7C
Revilla Gigedo, Islas MEXICO 12C
Reykjavik ICELAND 21B 30A
Réunion (FRANCE) 43D
Rhein, River GERMANY 31C 34B
Ribeirâo Preto BRAZIL 15C 17A
Richfield U.S.A 10B
Richmond U.S.A. 11D
Riga LATVIA 31D 32A
Rio Branco BRAZIL 14D
Río Colorado ARGENTINA 16D
Río Cuarto ARGENTINA 16D
Río Gallegos ARGENTINA 18A
Rio Grande BRAZIL 17C
Rio Grande U.S.A. 12A 10D
Rio Grande do Norte BRAZIL 15B 25C
Rio Grande do Sul BRAZIL 17A
Rio de Janeiro BRAZIL 15C 17A
Río Negro ARGENTINA 16D
Rio Negro BRAZIL 13D 14B
Río de la Plata 17C
Riobamba ECUADOR 14A

Riyadh SAUDI ARABIA 38B
Roanoke U.S.A. 11D
Robson, Mt. CANADA 7C
Rochester U.S.A. 8D 11B
Rockall (U.K.) 21B 30C
Rockhampton AUSTRALIA 63D 65B
Rocky Mountains CANADA 7C
Rocky Mountains U.S.A 7D 10B
Ródos GREECE 35C 37B 38A
Rodrigues I. MAURITIUS 59C
Romania 32C 35A
Rome ITALY 34D
Rondônia BRAZIL 14D
Rongelap At. 62A
Roosevelt I. ANTARCTICA 75D
Roraima BRAZIL 13D 14B
Rosario ARGENTINA 16D
Rose I. 70D
Roseau DOMINICA 13D
Ross Ice Shelf ANTARCTICA 75D
Ross Sea 75D
Rossija 46C
Rostock GERMANY 31C 34B
Rostov-na-Donu RUSSIA 32D 35B
Rota 62C
Rothera (U.K.) ANTARCTICA 18D 75C
Roti INDONESIA 61C
Rotorua N.Z. 66B
Rotterdam NETHERLANDS 30D 34B
Rouen FRANCE 30D 34A
Rovaniemi FINLAND 31B
Rovno UKRAINE 31D 32C 35A
Rowley I. CANADA 5C
Rudnaja Pristan SIBERIA 54D
Rurutu 71A
Ruse BULGARIA 32C 35C
Ruwenzori Mts. ZAIRE 40B
Rwanda 41C 42B
Rybinsk RUSSIA 32A 35B
Rybinskoje Vdchr. RUSSIA 32B
Ryukyu Islands JAPAN 55D

S

Saaremaa 31D 32A 35A
Sabhah LIBYA 37A
Sable I. CANADA 9D
Sable, I. de 63B 65B
Sachs Harbour CANADA 3B
Sachty RUSSIA 32D
Sacramento U.S.A. 10A
Sadiya INDIA 56B
Safi MOROCCO 23D 34C 36A
Saharanpur INDIA 56A
Sahel MALI 36D
Sahel NIGER 37C 40A
St. Anthony CANADA 9D
St. Anthony Newfoundland, CANADA 22A
St. Augustine U.S.A 13A 11D
St. Barthélemy (FRANCE) 13B
St. Christopher and Nevis 13B
St. Denis Réunion (FRANCE) 43D
St. George's GRENADA 13D 14B
St. Helena (U.K.) 25B 27A
St. Jean, L. CANADA 9C
St. John CANADA 9C
St. John's ANTIGUA AND BARBUDA 13B
St. John's Newfoundland, CANADA 9D 22A
St. Lawrence I. Alaska, U.S.A. 2C
St. Lawrence River CANADA 9C 11B
St. Lawrence River U.S.A. 11B
St. Lawrence, G. of CANADA 9D
St. Louis SENEGAL 24A 36C
St. Louis U.S.A. 8C 11A
Saint Lucia 13D
St. Paul I. (FRANCE) 59B
St. Paul U.S.A. 8C 11A
St. Pedro Sula HONDURAS 12D
St. Petersburg RUSSIA see Leningrad
St. Petersburg U.S.A. 11D 12B
St. Pierre-et-Miquelon (FRANCE) 9D 22A
St. Vincent and the Grenadines 13D
Saipan 62C
Saïda ALGERIA 34C
Sakisima Syoto JAPAN 55D
Sal'm O. FRANZ JOSEF LAND 29B
Sala y Gómez, I. (CHILE) 73D
Salado, River ARGENTINA 16B
Salado, River ARGENTINA 16D
Salalah OMAN 39C
Salayar INDONESIA 61C
Salechard SIBERIA 46C 74B
Salem U.S.A. 7C 10A
Salisbury I. CANADA 9A
Salomon I. 58D
Salta ARGENTINA 16B
Saltillo MEXICO 10D 12A
Salto URAGUAY 17C
Salvador BRAZIL 15D 25C
Salween, River BURMA 60A
Salzburg AUSTRIA 31C 34B
Samarkand UZBEKHISTAN 33D 39B
Samch'ok SOUTH KOREA 55C
Samsun TURKEY 32D 35D
S. Antonio U.S.A. 10D
San Antonio, C. ARGENTINA 17C
S. Antonio Oeste ARGENTINA 16D
S. Bernardino U.S.A. 10C
San Benedicto, I. MEXICO 12C
San Cristobal SOLOMON ISLANDS 63A
San Cristóbal VENEZUELA 13C 14A
San Cristóbal, I., Galápagos Islands 12D
San Diego U.S.A 10C
San Francisco U.S.A. 10A
San Jorge, G. 16D 18A
San Jose U.S.A. 10A
San José COSTA RICA 12D
San Juan ARGENTINA 16B
S. Juan Puerto Rico 13A
San Luis ARGENTINA 16D
S. Luis Potosi MEXICO 12A
S. Marino 34D
San Martin (ARGENTINA) 18D
San Matiás, G. 16D
S. Miguel de Tucumán ARGENTINA 16B
San-Pédro IVORY COAST 24B 36D
San Rafael ARGENTINA 16D
San Salvador GUATEMALA 12D
S. Salvador de J. ARGENTINA 16B
S. Sebastian SPAIN 23B 34C
San'a YEMEN 38D 41B
Sta. Barbara U.S.A 10C
Sta. Catarina BRAZIL 17A
Santa Clara CUBA 13A
Santa Cruz ARGENTINA 18A
Santa Cruz BOLIVIA 14D 16B
Sta. Cruz, I., Galápagos Islands 12D
Santa Cruz de Tenerife Canary Islands (SPAIN) 23C 36A
Santa Cruz Is. SOLOMON ISLANDS 63A
Santa Fe ARGENTINA 16B
Santa Fe U.S.A. 10D
Sta. Inés CHILE 18A
Santa Isabel SOLOMON ISLANDS 63A
Santa Maria BRAZIL 17A
Santa Rosa ARGENTINA 16D
Sta. Rosalía MEXICO 10C
Santarém BRAZIL 15A
Santarskije O-va SIBERIA 54C
Santiago CHILE 16D
Santiago DOMINICAN REPUBLIC 13A
Santiago de Cuba CUBA 13A
Santiago del Estero ARGENTINA 16B
Santo Antão CAPE VERDE 24C
Sto. Domingo DOMINICAN REPUBLIC 13A
Santos BRAZIL 17A
São José do Rio Preto BRAZIL 15C 17A
São Luis BRAZIL 15A
São Miguel, I. (PORTUGAL) 23C
São Paulo BRAZIL 15C 17A
São Roque, C. de BRAZIL 25C
São Tiago CAPE VERDE 24C
São Tomé SÃO TOMÉ AND PRINCIPE 40A
São Tomé, C. de BRAZIL 15D 17B
Sao Tomé and Principe 40A
Sape INDONESIA 61C
Sapporo JAPAN 54B
Saraburi THAILAND 57C 60A
Sarajevo YUGOSLAVIA 32C 35C
Saransk RUSSIA 32B 35B
Saratov RUSSIA 32D 35B
Sardegna ITALY 34D
Sardinia see Sardegna
Sargasso Sea 13B
Sarh CHAD 37C 40B
Sarja RUSSIA 32B
Saskatchewan CANADA 7D 8A
Saskatchewan, River CANADA 7D 8A
Saskatoon CANADA 7D 8A

Saudi Arabia 38B
Sault Ste Marie CANADA 8D 11B
Saunders I. 19B
Saurimo ANGOLA 40D
Savaii WEST SAMOA 70D
Savannah U.S.A. 11D 13A
Savannakhet LAOS 57C
Say'un YEMEN 38D 41B
Saynshand MONGOLIA 53C
Schefferville CANADA 9A
Scott (N.Z.) ANTARCTICA 75B
Scranton U.S.A. 8D 11B
Seattle U.S.A. 7C 10A
Ségou MALI 24A 36D
Sekondi-Takoradi GHANA 36D
Selagskij, M. SIBERIA 2A 49A
Selat Makasar INDONESIA 61C
Selat Sunda 60D
Semarang INDONESIA 60D
Semipalatinsk KAZAKHSTAN 52C
Sendai JAPAN 55A
Senegal 24A 36C
Sénégal, River SENEGAL 24A
Senyavin Is. 62B
Seoul SOUTH KOREA 55C
Sept-Iles CANADA 9C
Seram INDONESIA 61D
Sergeja, Kirova O-va SIBERIA 46A
Sergino SIBERIA 33A
Sergipe BRAZIL 15D
Sevastopol' CRIMEA 32D 35B
Sevcenko KAZAKHSTAN 33C
Severo Sibirskaja Nizmennost' SIBERIA 46D
Sevilla SPAIN 23D 34C
Seward Alaska, U.S.A. 2D 6B
Seychelles 41D 43B
Seydisfjördur ICELAND 21B 30A
Sfax TUNISIA 34D 37A
Shanghai CHINA 55D 57B
Shannon Ø GREENLAND 20B
Shansi CHINA 53D
Shantou CHINA 55D 57B
Shantung CHINA 55C 57B
Shaoguan CHINA 55D 57B
Shaoyang CHINA 57B
Shashemene ETHIOPIA 38D 41A
Sheffield U.K. 30D 34A
Shelikof Str. Alaska, U.S.A. 6A
Shensi CHINA 57A
Sherbrooke CANADA 9C
Shetland Is. (U.K.) 30B
Shihezi CHINA 52D
Shijiazhuang CHINA 53D
Shillong INDIA 56B
Shiquanhe CHINA 56A
Shiraz 39A
Shizuishan CHINA 53C
Shreveport U.S.A. 11C 12B
Siberia 74A
Siberut INDONESIA 60C
Sibir'akova, O. SIBERIA 46C
Sibu MALAYSIA 60D
Sicilia 34D 37A
Sierra Leone 24B 36C
Sierra Madre Occident MEXICO 10D 12A
Sierra Madre Orient MEXICO 10D 12A
Signy ((U.K.) ANTARCTICA 19C 75C
Sikkim 56B
Sikoku JAPAN 55A
Sikotan, O. SIBERIA 54B
Sikt'ach SIBERIA 47B
Simeulue INDONESIA 60C
Simla INDIA 56A
Simusir, O. SIBERIA 51C 54B
Sinai EGYPT 38A
Singapore 60D
Sinkiang CHINA 52D
Sintang INDONESIA 60D
Sioux City U.S.A. 8C 11A
Sioux Falls U.S.A. 8C 11A
Siping CHINA 54D
Sisimiut (Holsteinsborg) GREENLAND 5D 21C
Sitka Alaska, U.S.A. 6B
Sittwe BURMA 56D 60A
Sivas TURKEY 32D 35D
Skagway Alaska, U.S.A. 7A
Skien NORWAY 31C
Skopje YUGOSLAVIA 32C 35C
Skovorodino SIBERIA 53B 54C
Smidta, O. SIBERIA 46A
Smithton Tasmania, AUSTRALIA 66D
Smolensk RUSSIA 31D 32A 35B
Snake River U.S.A. 10A
Soci RUSSIA 32D 35D
Socorro, I. MEXICO 12C
Socotra YEMEN 39C
Sofia BULGARIA 32C 35C
Sokoto NIGERIA 40A 36D
Solapur INDIA 56C
Solimões, River BRAZIL 14B
Solomon Islands 63A
Solomon Sea 63C
Somalia 41B
Somerset I. CANADA 4D
Songea TANZANIA 41C 43A
Songkhla THAILAND 60A
Sonsorol Is. 61B
Sorol At. 61B 62D
Sorong INDONESIA 61D
Sous-le-Vent, Iles Iles de la Société 70B
Sousse TUNISIA 34D 37A
South Africa 27B 42D
South Atlantic Ocean 26C 26D
South Australia AUSTRALIA 64D
South Carolina U.S.A. 11D
South China Sea 57D 60B
South Dakota U.S.A. 8C 11A
South East Cape Tasmania, AUSTRALIA 66D
South Georgia (U.K.) 19B
South Island N.Z. 66B
South Korea 55C
South Lake Tahoe U.S.A. 10A
South Magnetic Pole 75B
South Orkney Is. ANTARCTICA 19C 75C
South Pacific Ocean 66A 72C
South Pole 75A
South Sandwich Group (U.K.) 19B
South Shetland Is. ANTARCTICA 18D 75C
Southampton I. CANADA 4D
Southampton U.K. 23B 30D 34A
Southport AUSTRALIA 65D 66C
Sovetskaja Gavan' SIBERIA 54B
Spain 23B
Spence Bay CANADA 4D
Spitzbergen (NORWAY) 28B
Spokane U.S.A. 7C 10A
Spratly I. CHINA 57D 60B
Springbok S.A. 27B 42C
Springfield U.S.A. 11A
Springfield U.S.A. 11C
Springs S.A. 42D
Sredinnyj Chrebet SIBERIA 49D
Srednekolymsk SIBERIA 48B
Sretensk SIBERIA 53B
Sri Lanka 56C 58A
Srinagar Kashmir, INDIA 39B 56A
Stanley Falkland Islands 18B
Stanovoj Chrebet SIBERIA 53B 54C
Starbuck I. 70A
Stavropol' RUSSIA 32D
Stefansson I. CANADA 4B
Sterlitamak RUSSIA. 33A
Stewart CANADA 7A
Stewart I. N.Z. 67A
Stockholm SWEDEN 31C
Stolbovoj, O. SIBERIA 47B
Store Koldewey Ø GREENLAND 20B
Stranraer U.K. 30D 34A
Strasbourg FRANCE 30D 34B
Stuttgart GERMANY 31C 34B
Suchumi GEORGIA 35D
Sucre BOLIVIA 14D 16B
Sudan 37D 38C 40B
Sudbury CANADA 8D 11B
Suez EGYPT 35D 37B 38A
Sukkur PAKISTAN 39B
Sula Kep.INDONESIA 61C
Sulawesi see Celebes
Sulu Arch. PHILIPPINES 61A
Sulu Sea 57D 61A
Sumatra INDONESIA 60C
Sumba INDONESIA 61C
Sumbawa INDONESIA 61C
Sumy UKRAINE 31D 32D 35B
Sundsvaal SWEDEN 31A
Suntar SIBERIA 47D 48C
Superior, L. CANADA 8D 11B
Superior, L. U.S.A. 8D 11B
Sur OMAN 39C
Surabaya 60D
Surat INDIA 39D 56C
Surat Thani THAILAND 60A
Surgut SIBERIA 33B
Suriname 13D 14B
Surt LIBYA 35C 37A
Susuman SIBERIA 49C
Suvadiva At. 58C
Suwarrow At. 70D
Suzhou CHINA 55D

INDEX

ABAB
CDCD

57B
Svalbard (NORWAY) 28B
74B
Sverdrup Islands CANADA
5A
Sverdrup Ø GREENLAND
20C
Swains I. 70D
Swaziland 42D
Sweden 28D
31A
34B
74B
Switzerland 31C
34B
Sydney AUSTRALIA 65C
66C
Sydney CANADA 9D
Syktyvkar RUSSIA 32B
74B
Syowa (JAPAN)
ANTARCTICA 44C
75A
Syracuse U.S.A. 8D
11B
Syrdarja, River
KAZAKHSTAN 33D
Syria 35D
38B
Szczecin POLAND 31C
Szechwan CHINA 57A

T

T'umen' SIBERIA 33B
Ta'izz YEMEN 38B
41B
Tabriz IRAN 33C
38B
Tacna PERU 14C
16A
Tacoma U.S.A. 7C
10A
Tadzhikistan 33D
52C
Taegu SOUTH KOREA 55C
Taejon SOUTH KOREA 55C
Tagula 63C
Tahe CHINA 53B
54C
Tahoua NIGER 36D
Tailem Bend AUSTRALIA
65C
Taipei TAIWAN 55D
57B
Taitao, Pen. de CHILE 18A
Taiwan 55D
57B
Taiwan Str. 55D
57B
Taiyuan CHINA 53D
Taj Mahal INDIA 56A
Tajo, River SPAIN 23D
34C
Tajset SIBERIA. 52B
Taklimakan Shamo CHINA
52D
Tallahassee U.S.A. 11D
12B
Tallinn ESTONIA 31D
32A
Tamale GHANA 24B
Tamanghasset ALGERIA
36B
Tambacounda SENEGAL
24A
36C
Tambov RUSSIA 32B
35B
Tamil Nadu INDIA 56C
Tampa U.S.A. 11D
12B
Tampere FINLAND 31B
32A
Tampico MEXICO 12A
Tanaga I. Alaska, U.S.A. 50B
Tanami Desert AUSTRALIA
64B
Tanana Alaska, U.S.A. 2D
Tandil ARGENTINA 16D
Tanezrouft ALGERIA 36B
Tanga TANZANIA 41C
43A
Tanganyika, L. TANZANIA
41C
Tanganyika, L. ZAIRE 42B
Tanger MOROCCO 23D
34C
36B
Tangshan CHINA 53D
55C
Tanimbar, Kep.
INDONESIA 61D
Tanna VANUATU 63B
Tanzania 41C
43A
Taolagnaro MADAGASCAR
43D
Taongi At. 62A
Tapachula MEXICO 12D
Tapajos, River BRAZIL 15A
Tara SIBERIA 33B
52A
Tarawa At. 62B
Tarfaya MOROCCO 23D
36A
Tarim, River CHINA 52D
Tarko-Sale SIBERIA 46D
Taskent 33D
52C
Tasman Sea 66B
Tasmania 66D
Tatakoto 72A
Tatarskij Proliv 54A
Tavoy BURMA 57C
60A
Taxco MEXICO 12A
Tbilisi GEORGIA 32D
Tegucigalpa HONDURAS
12D
Tehran IRAN 39A
Tehuantepec MEXICO 12C
Tel Aviv ISRAEL 35D
38A
Teles Pires, River BRAZIL
14D
Telukbetung INDONESIA
60D
Temirtau KAZAKHSTAN
33D
52C
Temuco CHILE 16C
Tenerife Canary Islands
(SPAIN) 23C
36A
Tennant Creek AUSTRALIA
64B
Tennessee U.S.A. 11C
Teotihuacán, Mt. MEXICO
12A
Teófilo Otoni BRAZIL 15D
17B
Tepic MEXICO 12A
Tequl'det SIBERIA 52B
Teraina 69B
Terceira, I. (PORTUGAL)
23C
Teresina BRAZIL 15B
Tete MOZAMBIQUE 41C
43A
Teuco, River ARGENTINA
16B
Texas U.S.A 12A
11C
Ténéré NIGER 37C
Thailand 57C
60A
Thanh Hoa VIETNAM 57C
Thessaloniki GREECE 32C
35C
Thimbu BHUTAN 56B
Thompson CANADA 8A
Thule Is. 19D
Thunder Bay CANADA 8D
11A
Thurso U.K. 30D
34A
Thurston I. ANTARCTICA
75D
Tian Shan CHINA 52D
Tianshui CHINA 57A
Tibesti CHAD 37A
Tibet CHINA 56B
Tierra del Fuego
ARGENTINA 18B
Tigris, River IRAQ 38B
Tijuana MEXICO 10C
Tiksi SIBERIA 47B
Timbuktu see Tombouctou
Timisoara ROMANIA 32C
35A
Timmins CANADA 8D
11B
Timor INDONESIA 61C
Timor Sea 61C
Tindouf ALGERIA 23D
Tinian 62C
Tintsin CHINA 53D
55C
Tirane ALBANIA 32C
35C
Tiruchchirappalli INDIA 56C
Titicaca, L. BOLIVIA 14D
16B
Titicaca, L. PERU 14D
16B
Titograd YUGOSLAVIA 32C
35C
Tlemcen ALGERIA 23D
34C
Toamasina MADAGASCAR
41D
43B
Tobago TRINIDAD AND
TOBAGO 13D
Tobago, I. TRINIDAD AND
TOBAGO 14B
Tobol'sk SIBERIA 33B
Tocantinopolis BRAZIL 15C
Tocantins BRAZIL 15C
Tocantins, River BRAZIL
15A
Togo 36D
Toili INDONESIA 61C
Tok Alaska, U.S.A. 2D
6B
Tokelau Is. (NEW
ZEALAND) 70C
Tokyo JAPAN 55A
Toledo U.S.A. 8D
11B
Toliara MADAGASCAR 43C
Toljatti RUSSIA 33A
Toluca MEXICO 12A
Tombouctou MALI 24A
36D
Tommot SIBERIA 48C
53B
Tomsk SIBERIA 52A
Tonga 71C
Tonga Trench 70D
Tongatapu Group 71C
Tonghua CHINA 55C
Topeka U.S.A. 8C
11A
Torino ITALY 34B
Toronto CANADA 8D
11B
Torreón MEXICO 10D
12A
Torres Strait 63C
Toubkal, J. MOROCCO 23D
34C
36A
Toulouse FRANCE 34C
Tours FRANCE 30D
34A
Townsville AUSTRALIA 63D
65A
Trabzon TURKEY 32D
35D
Traill Ø GREENLAND 21A
Trenton U.S.A. 9C
11B
Trieste ITALY 34B
Trincomalee SRI LANKA
56C
Trinidad TRINIDAD AND
TOBAGO 13D
14B
Trinidade (BRAZIL) 15D
17B
25D
26A
Tripoli LIBYA 34D
37A
Tristan da Cunha I. (U.K.)
26D
Trivandrum INDIA 56C
58A
Troicko-Pecorsk RUSSIA
33A
Trois-Rivières CANADA 9C
Tromelin I. (FRANCE) 41D
43B
Tromsø NORWAY 28D
31A
Trondheim NORWAY 31A
Tropolitania LIBYA 34D
37A
Trujillo PERU 14C
Truk Is. 62D
**Trust Terrritory of the
Pacific Islands** (U.S.A.)
62A
Tsaratanana
MADAGASCAR 41D
43B
Tsinghai CHINA 53C
56B
Tsumeb Namibia, S.A. 27B

42A
Tuamotu Islands 70B 72A
Tubuai 71A
Tucson U.S.A. 10D
Tuktoyaktuk CANADA 3D
Tula RUSSIA 32B 35B
Tulsa U.S.A. 11C
Tunguska, Niz, River SIBERIA 47C
Tunis TUNISIA 34D 37A
Tunisia 34D 37A
Tura SIBERIA 47C
Turkey 32D 35D 38A
Turkmen Rep. 33C 39A
Turks and Caicos Is. BAHAMAS 13A
Turku FINLAND 31B 32A
Turpan CHINA 52D
Turuchansk SIBERIA 46D
Tutuala Timor INDONESIA 61C
Tutuila WEST SAMOA 70D
Tuxtla Gutiérrez MEXICO 12B
Tynda SIBERIA 53B 54C
Tyrrhenian Sea 34D

U
Ua Huka 72A
Ua Pu 72A
Ubangui, River ZAIRE 37D 40B
Uberaba BRAZIL 15C 17A
Uberlândia BRAZIL 15C 17A
Ucayali, River PERU 14C
Uchta RUSSIA 33A
Udaipur INDIA 39B 56A
Udon Thani THAILAND 57C 60A
Uelen SIBERIA 2A
Ufa RUSSIA 33A
Uganda 41A
Ujjain INDIA 39B 56A
Ujung Pandang INDONESIA 61C
Ukraine 31D 32C 35A
Ulan Bator MONGOLIA 53C
Ulan-Ude SIBERIA 53A
Uliga Majuro At. 62B
Ulithi Atoll 61B 62C
Umeå SWEDEN 31A
Umnak I. ALASKA 50B
Umtata S.A. 42D
Unalakleet Alaska, U.S.A. 2C
Unalaska I. Alaska, U.S.A. 50A
Ungava Bay 9A
Unimak I. Alaska, U.S.A. 50A
United Arab Emirates 39A
United Kingdom 23B 30D 34A
United States of America 10B 10D 11A 11C
Upernavik GREENLAND 20D
Upington S.A. 42D
Upolu WEST SAMOA 70D
Uppsala SWEDEN 31C
Ural Mountains 33A 74B
Ural'sk KAZAKHSTAN 33A
Ural, River RUSSIA 33A
Uranium City CANADA 7B 8A
Uruguaiana BRAZIL 17A
Uruguay 17C
Uruguay, River BRAZIL 17A
Urumchi CHINA 52D
Urup, O. SIBERIA 54B
Usakova, O. SIBERIA 46A
Ushuaia ARGENTINA 18A
Ussurijsk SIBERIA 54D
Ust'-Bol'sereck SIBERIA 54A
Ust'-Kamcatsk SIBERIA 49D 50D
Ust'Kamenogorsk KAZAKHSTAN 52C
Ust'-Kujga SIBERIA 48A
Ust'-Kut SIBERIA 53A
Ust'-Nera SIBERIA 48D 74A
Utah U.S.A. 10B
Utirik At. 62A
Uttar Pradesh INDIA 56A
Utunomiya JAPAN 55A
Uummannaq GREENLAND 21C
Uzbekistan 33D
Uzogorsk RUSSIA 32B

V
Vaal, River S.A. 42D
Vaasa FINLAND 32A
Vadodara INDIA 39D
Vail U.S.A. 10B
Valdez Alaska, U.S.A. 2D 6B
Valdés , Pen. ARGENTINA 16D
Valdivia CHILE 16C
Valencia SPAIN 23D 34C
Valencia VENEZUELA 14B
Valladolid SPAIN 23B
Valletta MALTA 34D 37A
Valleyview CANADA 7D
Valparaiso CHILE 16C
Van TURKEY 32D 35D 38B
Vancouver CANADA 7C 10A
Vancouver I. CANADA 7C 10A
Vanern SWEDEN 31A
Vanua Levu 70D
Vanuatu 63B
Varna BULGARIA 32C 35C
Vatican City ITALY 34D
Vättern SWEDEN 31C 34B
Vava'u Group 70D
Velikije Luki RUSSIA 31D 32A 35A
Venezia ITALY 34B
Venezuela 13D 14B
Veracruz MEXICO 12A
Verchojansk SIBERIA 48A 74A
Verchojanskij Chrebet SIBERIA 48A
Vereeniging S.A. 42D
Vermont U.S.A. 9C
Vert, C. SENEGAL 24A 36C
Vesterålen NORWAY 28D 31A
Vestspitzbergen NORWAY 28B
Vesuvio ITALY 34D
Victoria AUSTRALIA 65C 66C
Victoria CANADA 7C 10A
Victoria Falls ZIMBABWE 40D 42B
Victoria Fjord GREENLAND 20C
Victoria I. CANADA 4C 74C
Victoria Land ANTARCTICA 75B
Victoria Mahé I. SEYCHELLES 41D 43B
Victoria, L. KENYA 41A
Victoria, L. TANZANIA 41C
Viedma ARGENTINA 16D
Vienna AUSTRIA 31C 34B
Vientiane LAOS 57C 60A
Vietnam 57C 60B
Vigo SPAIN 23B 34C
Vijayawada INDIA 56C
Vil'kickogo, O. SIBERIA 46C
Vil'kickogo, Pr. 46B
Vil'uj, River SIBERIA 47D
Vil'ujsk SIBERIA 48C
Vila VANUATU 63B
Villa María ARGENTINA 16D
Villahermosa MEXICO 12B
Villarica PARAGUAY 17A
Vilnius LITHUANIA 31D 32A 35A
Vinnica UKRAINE 31D 32C 35A
Vinson Massif ANTARCTICA 75C
Virgin Is. (U.K.) 13B
Virginia U.S.A. 11D
Viscount Melville Sound 4B
Vitebsk BYELORUSSIA 31D 32A
Vitória da Conquista BRAZIL 15D 17B
Vladimir RUSSIA 32B 35B
Vladiv.. tok SIBERIA 54D
Volga, River RUSSIA 32A 32B 32D
Volgograd RUSSIA 32D
Vologda RUSSIA 32B
Volta GHANA 36D
Vorkuta RUSSIA 46C
Voronez RUSSIA 32D 35B
Vorosilovgrad UKRAINE 32D 35B
Vostok 75B
Vostok I. 70B
Vrangel'a, O. SIBERIA 2A
Vyborg U.S.S.R. 31B 32A

W
Waco U.S.A 12A 11C
Wad Madani SUDAN 37D 38C 41A
Wadi Halfa SUDAN 37B 38C
Waigeo INDONESIA 61D
Wake (U.S.A.) 62A
Wakkanai JAPAN 54B
Wales Alaska, U.S.A. 2C
Wales I. CANADA 4D
Wallis, I. (FRANCE) 70D
Walvisbaai Namibia (S.A.) 27B 42C
Wanxian CHINA 57A
Warsaw POLAND 31C 32C 35A
Washington U.S.A. 8D 11B
Washington State U.S.A. 7C 10A
Watson Lake CANADA 7A
Waw SUDAN 37D 38C 40B
Weddell Sea 19C 75C
Weifang CHINA 53D 55C
Wellesley Is. AUSTRALIA 63D 65A
Wellington N.Z. 66B
Wellington, I. CHILE 18A
Wenzhou CHINA 55D 57B
West Antarctica 75D
West Bengal INDIA 56B
West Ice Shelf ANTARCTICA 45D
West Palm Beach U.S.A 13A 11D
West Samoa 70D

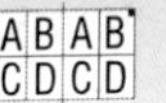

West Siberian Plain 33B 52A
W Virginia U.S.A. 11B
Western Sahara 23D 24A 36A
Westport N.Z. 66B
Wetar INDONESIA 61C
Wewak P.N.G. 63C
White Nile, River SUDAN 37D 38C 41A
White Sea 29C
Whitehorse CANADA 3C 7A 74C
Whitney, Mt. U.S.A. 10C
Whyalla AUSTRALIA 64D
Wichita U.S.A. 11C
Wilkes Land ANTARCTICA 75B
Willemstad CURAÇAO 13C 14A
Williamsburg U.S.A. 11D
Wilmington U.S.A. 11D
Windhoek Namibia, S.A. 27B 42C
Winnemucca U.S.A. 10A
Winnipeg CANADA 8C 11A
Winnipeg, L. CANADA 8A
Winton AUSTRALIA 63D 65A
Wisconsin U.S.A. 8C 11A
Wista, River POLAND 31C 32C 35A
Wollongong AUSTRALIA 65C 66C
Woods, L. of the CANADA 8C 11A
Worcester S.A. 42D
Worcester U.S.A. 9C
Wotje At. 62A
Wroclaw POLAND 31C 35A
Wuhan CHINA 55D 57B
Wuhu CHINA 55D 57B
Wuwei CHINA 53C 57A
Wuzhou CHINA 57B
Wyndham AUSTRALIA 64B
Wyoming U.S.A 10B

X
Xi Jiang, River CHINA 57D
Xi'an CHINA 57A
Xiagntan CHINA 57B
Xiamen CHINA 55B 57B
Xichang CHINA 57A
Xigaze CHINA 56B
Xilinhot CHINA 53D
Xingtai CHINA 53D 57B
Xining CHINA 53C 57A
Xinyang CHINA 57B
Xuzhou CHINA 55C 57B

Y
Yalta see Jalta
Yamoussoukro IVORY COAST 24B 36D
Yan'an CHINA 57A
Yangon (Rangoon) BURMA 56D 60A
Yangtze, River CHINA 57A
Yanji CHINA 54D
Yantai CHINA 55C
Yaoundé CAMEROON 37C 40A
Yap 61B 62C
Yapen INDONESIA 61D
Yaren NAURU 62B
Yarmouth CANADA 9C
Yazd IRAN 39A
Yellow River CHINA 57A
Yellow Sea 55C 57B
Yellowknife CANADA 3D 7B 74C
Yellowstone Nat. Park U.S.A. 10B
Yemen 38D 41B
Yichang CHINA 57B
Yinchuan CHINA 53C
Yogyakarta INDONESIA 60D
Yokohama JAPAN 55A
York. C. AUSTRALIA 63C
York, Capé, Peninsula AUSTRALIA 63C 64A
Yorkton CANADA 7D 8A
Yucatán MEXICO 12B
Yugoslavia 32C 35C
Yukon Territory CANADA 3C 7A
Yukon, River Alaska, U.S.A. 2D
Yukon, River CANADA 7A 3C 74C
Yulin CHINA 53D
Yumen CHINA 53C
Yunnan CHINA 57A

Z
Zagorsk RUSSIA 32B 35B
Zagreb YUGOSLAVIA 34B
Zahedan IRAN 39A
Zaire 40B 40D 42B
Zaire River, ZAIRE 42A 42B
Zajsan KAZAKHSTAN 52D
Zalantun CHINA 53D 54D
Zaliv Selichova 49C
Zambezi, River ZAMBIA 40D 42B
Zambezi, River MOZAMBIQUE 41C 43A
Zambia 40D
Zamboanga PHILIPPINES 61A
Zanzibar TANZANIA 43A
Zanzibar I. Zanzibar TANZANIA 41C 43A
Zaozhuang CHINA 55C 57B
Zapol'arnyj RUSSIA 29C 31B
Zaporozje UKRAINE 32D 35B
Zaragoza SPAIN 23B 34C
Zavodovski I. 19B
Zeml'a Aleksandry, O. FRANZ JOSEF LAND 29A
Zeml'a Georga FRANZ JOSEF LAND 29A
Zhangjiakou CHINA 53D
Zhanjiang CHINA 57D
Zhengzhou CHINA 57B
Zibo CHINA 53D 55C 57B
Zigansk SIBERIA 47D
Zihuatanejo MEXICO 12A
Zimbabwe 40D 42B
Zinder NIGER 37C 40A
Zitomir UKRAINE 31D 32C 35A
Zlatoust RUSSIA 33A
Zouar CHAD 37C
Zouérat MAURITANIA 24A 36A
Zunyi CHINA 57A
Zurich SWITZERLAND 31C
Zyr'anka SIBERIA 48B

Mapping © MICHELIN et CIE
Propriétaires-Editeurs 1991

Creation, graphic arrangement,
Index © I-Spy Limited 1991

Edited and designed by Curtis Garratt Limited, The Old Vicarage, Horton cum Studley, Oxford OX9 1BT

Planning George E Fowkes

MICHELIN ® and the Michelin Man are Registered Trademarks of Michelin

Colour reproduction by Norwich Litho Services Limited
Printed in Spain

ISBN 1 85671 089 0